Dr Gareth Moore is the author of over 50 puzzle and brain-training books for both children and adults, including *The Mammoth Book of Brain Games*, *The Mammoth Book of New Sudoku* and *The Mammoth Book of Fun Brain Training*. His puzzles also appear in a range of newspapers and magazines, and he frequently features in the media as a puzzle expert.

He is also the creator of the daily brain-training website *BrainedUp.com*, and runs popular puzzle site *PuzzleMix.com*.

Dr Gareth Moore

The

Mindfulness
Puzzle Book

ROBINSON

ROBINSON

First published in Great Britain in 2016 by Robinson

7 9 10 8

Copyright © Dr Gareth Moore, 2016

The moral right of the author has been asserted.

A CIP catalogue record for this book
is available from the British Library.

ISBN: 978-1-47213-750-0

Typeset in Palotino Linotype by Dr Gareth Moore
Printed and bound in Great Britain by CPI Group (UK), Croydon
CRO 4YY

Papers used by Robinson are from well-managed forests and other
responsible sources.

Robinson
An imprint of
Little, Brown Book Group
Carmelite House
50 Victoria Embankment
London EC4Y 0DZ

An Hachette UK Company
www.hachette.co.uk

www.littlebrown.co.uk

Contents

For my family

Introduction

It's time to sit back and relax, with this collection of restful puzzles and brain-training activities, designed to relieve stress and inspire creativity.

This book features a wide range of specially selected games to provide the perfect level of challenge and reward for your brain. Feel the tension release as you focus on each achievable and fun task, and experience the endorphin reward buzz as you successfully complete each puzzle. What's more, all of the puzzles in this book have been specially created to provide a balanced level of challenge, meaning that you should be able to make good progress on virtually all of the puzzles.

Stimulating your mind with each puzzle also helps unlock your brain's innate creativity, just as sleep and rest can help you reach a breakthrough on pending tasks. This book will help you feel refreshed and renewed, and ready to carry on with your daily life. It also includes some special creativity and memory tasks, to help you to challenge your brain and practise these key skills.

The puzzles include a wide selection of classic puzzle types that you will be familiar with, as well as a small number of types that you might not have come across before. None of the puzzles have complex rules, however, so it's best to give them all a go, and let your brain enjoy the reward of successfully solving a new type of problem! There are also some more grown-up versions of childhood classics, with mindful activities such as colouring patterns, mazes, dot-to-dots and even a couple of spot the differences.

Each puzzle should be solvable within a short break, so you don't need to set aside a lot of time to use this book. Just pick it up when you fancy a few minutes of mindful relaxation. And if you ever get stuck, just turn to the full solutions at the back to grab yourself a free hint!

So sit back, relax, and enjoy these mindfulness puzzles.

Dr Gareth Moore – mindfulness@drgarethmoore.com

Simple Sudoku

See how quickly you can complete these easy puzzles – just place the digits from 1 to 4 into every row, column and 2×2 box for each puzzle.

Puzzle 1

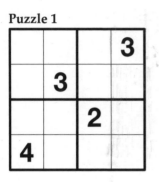

Puzzle 2

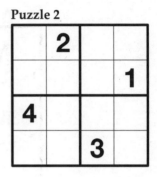

Puzzle 3

Puzzle 4

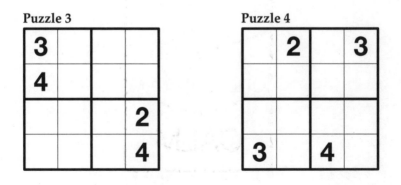

Some Rearrangement Required

Each of the following phrases can be rearranged to form the name of a sport. Can you solve them all?

A cherry

Bat on mind

My cats sign

Ignore in tree

Plot in margin

Tropical Dots

Join each of these dots in increasing numerical order, starting from 1, to reveal something you might find on a tropical island.

Placing Words

Fit all the listed words into the grid, crossword-style.

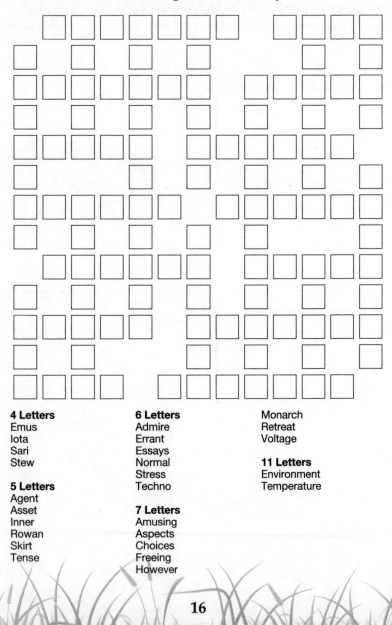

4 Letters
Emus
Iota
Sari
Stew

5 Letters
Agent
Asset
Inner
Rowan
Skirt
Tense

6 Letters
Admire
Errant
Essays
Normal
Stress
Techno

7 Letters
Amusing
Aspects
Choices
Freeing
However

Monarch
Retreat
Voltage

11 Letters
Environment
Temperature

Missing Details

Using your imagination, can you use a pen or pencil to convert these rectangles into pictures of four different **things you might find at home**? For example, one could be a goldfish tank and another could be a TV.

Colour by Illusion

It can be very relaxing to colour in an image, but if you colour in this pattern so that the circular shapes are darker than the backgrounds you'll also create an optical illusion.

Mini Crossword

Solve each of the clues to complete this mini-crossword grid.

Across
1 Elevators (5)
4 Living-room appliances (abbr) (3)
6 What we breathe (3)
7 Hard pull (3)
8 In the past (3)
9 Electrically charged particle (3)
10 Snakelike fish (3)
11 Adversary (5)

Down
1 Young (6)
2 Easily broken (7)
3 Bizarre (7)
5 Eerie (6)

Word Paths

How many words of three or more letters can you find in this square?
Find words by moving horizontally or vertically (but not diagonally)
from letter to touching letter, and without revisiting a square in a
single word. There is also one word that uses every letter.

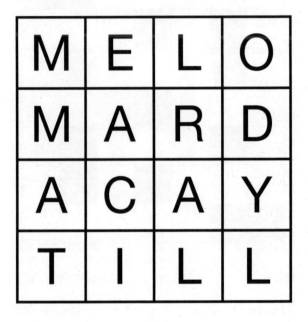

Fancy a challenge? If so, can you find 30 words?

Anagram Pairs

Draw lines to join each word in the left-hand column to a word in the right-hand column, where the two words are anagrams of one another. For example, you could join MELONS to LEMONS.

Angers	Feared
Ardent	Height
Avails	Itches
Burble	Peered
Deafer	Ranges
Deeper	Ranted
Eighth	Ravine
Erased	Recipe
Ethics	Rename
Impure	Rubble
Meaner	Saliva
Naiver	Seared
Pierce	Souped
Pseudo	Theses
Sheets	Umpire

Reverse Words

Can you solve each of the following clues? Each pair of clues reveal the same word, except that the solution to each 'b' clue is the **reverse** of the 'a' clue. For example, if the 'a' solution is DOG then the 'b' solution will be GOD, and vice versa.

Puzzle 1
a. Something given in recognition of an achievement
b. A slide-out storage compartment

Puzzle 2
a. A strip of material used to carry something
b. A set of components that can be assembled to form another object

Puzzle 3
a. A word that means 'fit for a monarch'
b. A type of beer

Puzzle 4
a. A location inside a building
b. Open, uncultivated land

Loop the Loop

Join all of the dots using only horizontal or vertical lines to form a single loop. The loop can only visit each dot once, and it can't cross over or touch itself at any point.

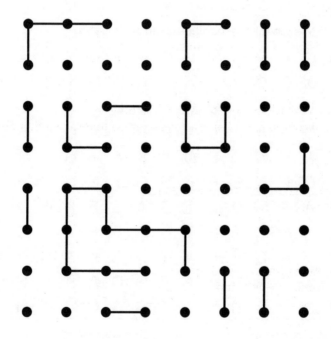

Look After Yourself

Can you find all of the listed words and phrases in the grid? They are written forwards or backwards in any direction, including diagonally.

```
N G O F O R A W A L K D P S T
D U R K W H R U N W I N D R P
F E O A O V A E L L T N H U F
G Y M W O R K O U T E C T F R
R C A P O M E B R I N Y O A E
N W O D R I A H R U O Y T E L
A F H F I B E F L U A A N T O
E O A A F L T R R D A O G F O
F R V W O E O F E A I G U O C
D O E K E F E H O T E N N P R
E A A M O E T B A B E K G U E
O O N G T E T C R E L A X C T
F M A U V L A Y N E K A O R A
N I P A N V A F G C A A D U W
K H H C O S I T B A C K T H E
```

COFFEE BREAK
CUP OF TEA
GO FOR A WALK
GO FOR LUNCH
GYM WORKOUT
HAVE A NAP
HAVE THE DAY OFF
LET YOUR HAIR DOWN

MEET FRIENDS
PUT YOUR FEET UP
RELAX
SIT BACK
TAKE A HOLIDAY
UNWIND
VACATION
WATER COOLER

Memory List

It's a good mindfulness technique to make a list of all the things you need to remember, so you don't worry about forgetting them. But this doesn't mean you should never exercise your memory!

Spend up to a minute remembering the groceries list below, then cover it over, wait a few seconds, and then see how many you can write out again in the gaps at the bottom of the page.

Toothpaste	Bread	Milk
Sugar	Eggs	Peppers
Cereal	Yoghurt	Cream
Celery	Beans	Kitchen towel

_____   _____   _____

_____   _____   _____

_____   _____   _____

_____   _____   _____

The Numbers Game

Can you form each of the three totals below, using all of the listed numbers just once each? For example, you could form a total of 31 by adding the 4 and 2, multiplying by 5, and then adding the remaining 1.

1   2   4   5

Totals:

29

38

44

Link Words

Find a common English word to place in each gap, so that both when attached to the end of the first word and when attached to the start of the second word you end up with two more English words. For example, **birth** _ _ _ **break** could be solved using **day**, making **birthday** and **daybreak**.

grab   _ _ _   room

dam   _ _ _ _   ion

tail   _ _ _ _   way

Just for Fun

See if you can come up with an amusing or witty conclusion to each of these partial jokes! There are no correct answers here – the idea is just to provide a bit of creative relaxation.

Did you hear about the penguin who went to the chemist?

_____

What happened when the red tour bus and the blue tour bus bumped into each other?

_____

Why did the panda, the fox, the horse and the monkey cross the road?

_____

Arrow Word

All of this crossword's clues are given inside the grid.

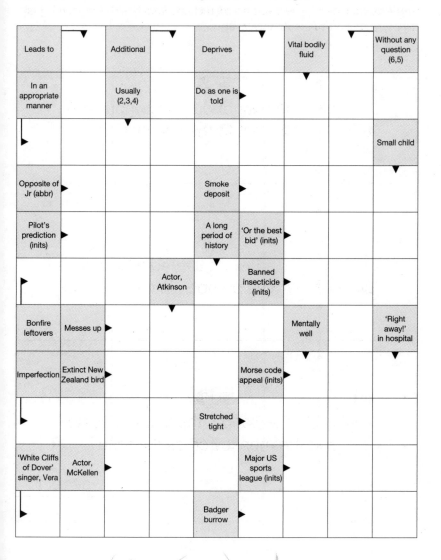

Brain Chains

Can you solve each of the three brain chains completely in your head, without making any written notes? Start with the bold number at the top, and then apply each maths operation in turn. Write your final result in at the bottom.

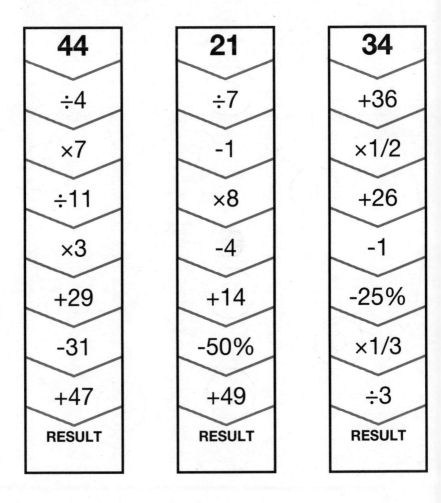

44	**21**	**34**
÷4	÷7	+36
×7	-1	×1/2
÷11	×8	+26
×3	-4	-1
+29	+14	-25%
-31	-50%	×1/3
+47	+49	÷3
RESULT	**RESULT**	**RESULT**

Word Orbit

By picking one letter from each orbit in turn, working in from the outermost ring to the innermost ring, how many four-letter words can you find?

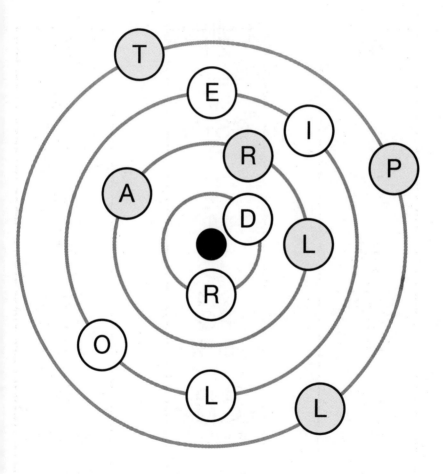

Missing Vowels

All of the vowels have been deleted from the following words. Can you restore them by working out what the original words were?

CLMBNG

QSTN

TRVLLY

PQ

MNMM

Hidden Path

Join some of the dots with horizontal and vertical lines to form a single path. The path should not touch or cross either itself or any of the solid blocks. Numbers outside the grid specify the exact number of dots in their row or column that are visited by the path. The start and end of the path are given to you, and are marked by the solid dots.

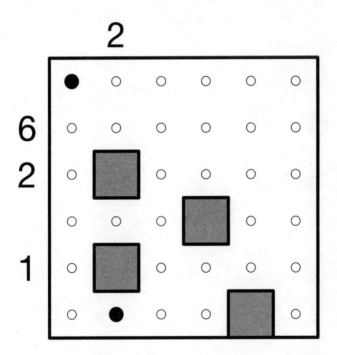

Sleeping Cats Lie

Can you find the six differences between these two images? Just to make it a little bit harder, one of the images is rotated half a revolution compared to the other.

Grid Memory

Look at the pattern in the grid at the top-left of the page, then cover it over and see if you can accurately reproduce it in the empty grid at the top-right of the page. Then repeat with each of the other two grids.

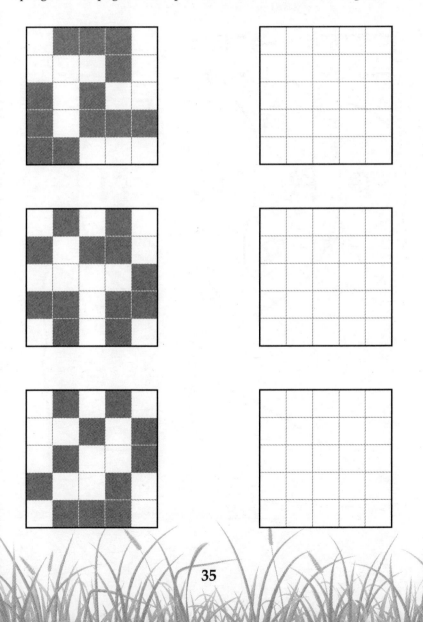

Letter Circle

How many words of three or more letters can you find in this letter circle? Each word should use the centre letter plus two or more of the other letters, and no letter can be used more than once in a single word. There is one word that uses every letter.

Fancy a challenge? If so, can you find 25 words?

Missing Signs

Give your mind a workout by writing the missing mathematical sign into each of these equations: +, −, × or ÷.

28 ☐ 6 = 22   63 ☐ 9 = 7

53 ☐ 6 = 59   45 ☐ 18 = 63

8 ☐ 35 = 43   11 ☐ 16 = 27

60 ☐ 5 = 12   9 ☐ 8 = 72

8 ☐ 10 = 80   11 ☐ 12 = 132

44 ☐ 4 = 11   40 ☐ 13 = 27

64 ☐ 16 = 48   35 ☐ 5 = 7

108 ☐ 9 = 12   9 ☐ 9 = 81

9 ☐ 2 = 18   11 ☐ 11 = 121

11 ☐ 5 = 55   3 ☐ 2 = 6

Dot Drawings

Try this creative task by drawing straight lines to join some, or all, of the dots together. See if you can come up with a pattern or picture, even with this restricted set of dots! Even if you have no idea what you want to draw, just start by joining dots at random and see what it begins to look like!

Shape Link

Draw a series of separate paths, each connecting a pair of identical shapes. Paths only travel horizontally or vertically, and they don't cross or touch at any point. No more than one path can enter any grid square.

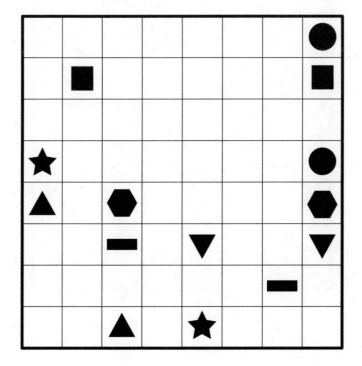

Never Four in a Row

Place either an 'X' or an 'O' into each empty square of this grid, so that **no rows of four or more** 'X's or 'O's are made in any direction, including diagonally.

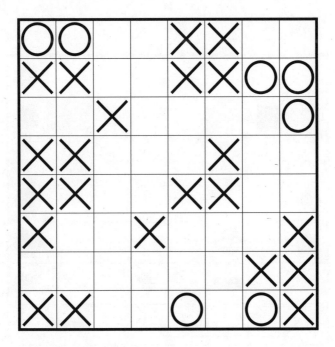

Misdirection

Does this pattern consist of lots of arrows pointing right, with gaps in between, or lots of arrows pointing left? Or both? It all depends on how you colour it in – and visualize it!

Missing Capitals

First, cover up the bottom of the page (below the dividing line), then spend up to a minute remembering the list of cities below, then cover it over, wait a few seconds, and then see if you can spot which ones are missing from the list at the bottom of the page.

Paris	London	Miami
Amsterdam	Kiev	Helsinki
San Francisco	Rio de Janeiro	Kuala Lumpur
Sofia	Beijing	Brussels
Athens	Istanbul	Ottawa

Amsterdam	Athens	Brussels
Helsinki	Istanbul	London
Ottawa	Paris	Sofia

_____ _____ _____

_____ _____ _____

Jigsaw Letters

To solve these puzzles, place a letter from A to E into each empty square so that every row, column and bold-lined jigsaw shape contains each letter exactly once.

Puzzle 1

		C		
				A
		B		
D				
		A		

Puzzle 2

A			C	
		E		
	B			D

Mini Crossword

Solve each of the clues to complete this mini-crossword grid.

Across
3 Large birds of prey (6)
4 Guitar loudspeaker (3)
5 Foundations (5)
7 Cuddly toy (abbr) (3)
8 Manually (2,4)

Down
1 Radio code word for 'P' (4)
2 Came to a halt (6)
3 Womb resident (6)
6 Highest European volcano (4)

Mental Maths

Massage your brain with these maths calculations – do as many as you can without using a calculator or making written notes.

$17 \times 5 =$ [ ]

$19 + 72 =$ [ ]

$8 + 51 =$ [ ]

$31 - 16 =$ [ ]

$14 \times 7 =$ [ ]

$8 + 29 =$ [ ]

$78 \div 2 =$ [ ]

$96 \div 12 =$ [ ]

$8 + 58 =$ [ ]

$174 \div 6 =$ [ ]

$35 - 13 =$ [ ]

$171 \div 3 =$ [ ]

$41 - 23 =$ [ ]

$56 - 21 =$ [ ]

$12 \times 3 =$ [ ]

$32 + 23 =$ [ ]

$32 - 13 =$ [ ]

$24 + 21 =$ [ ]

$71 + 14 =$ [ ]

$7 \times 16 =$ [ ]

Floating Flowers

Each of the following phrases can be rearranged to form the name of a flower. Can you solve them all?

DO RICH

MORE RIPS

RUIN GAME

SLOWER FUN

HIDE IN PLUM

Silhouette Selection

Which of the four silhouettes matches the leaves at the top of the page?

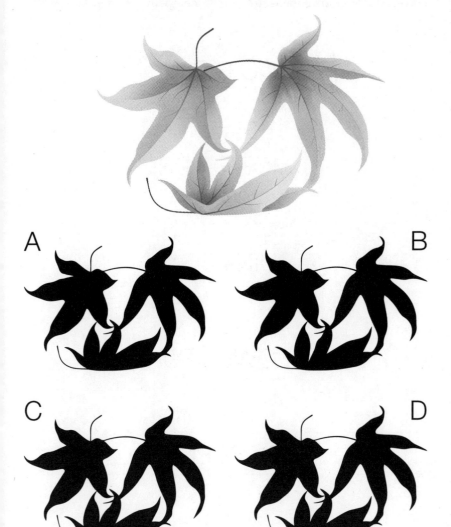

Classic Maze

Can you find your way through this square maze, travelling from the entrance at the top all the way down to the exit at the bottom?

Start and End

For each of these puzzles, add the same letter to both the start and end of the given fragment to form a normal English word. For example, add S to _TART_ to form STARTS.

NORE

OSEWATE

HEF

NCLOSUR

TAG

_WI_

AWNE

Image Combination

Imagine combining these two images, so each white square in one is filled with the contents of the corresponding square in the other image. How many circles would there be in total?

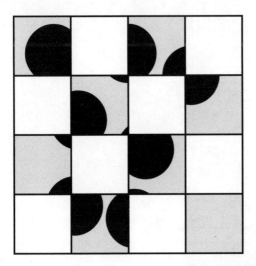

Arrow Word

All of this crossword's clues are given inside the grid.

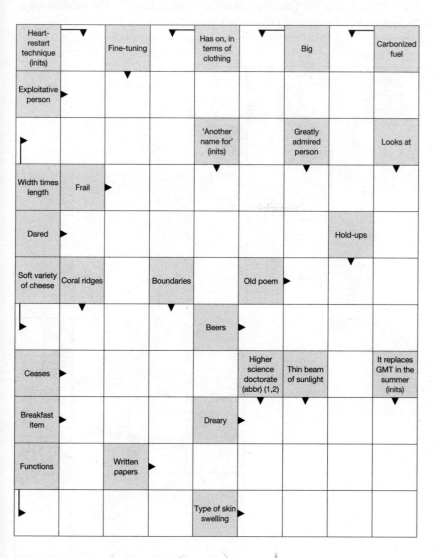

Cube Counting

How many individual cubes have been used to build the structure below? You should assume that all 'hidden' cubes are present, and that it started off as a perfect 5×4×4 arrangement of cubes (as shown to the right) before any cubes were removed. There are no floating cubes.

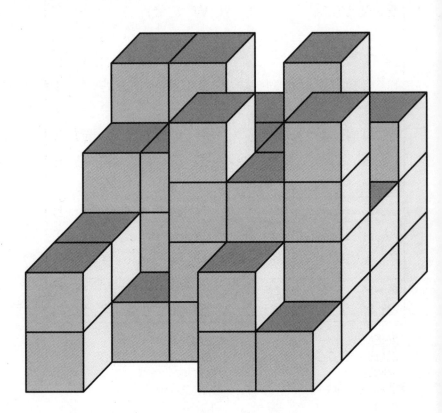

Leisure Activities

Can you find all of the listed entries in the grid? They are written forwards or backwards in any direction, including diagonally.

```
T N G A W A T C H I N G T V I
L G N I T T I N K S F N C R E
E A W M L E L R W L N O U I T
I C D S L S A I O I E H G T G
M T S A I E M G C S C I S K N
S C M E N M V E T T T E G C I
N P N G I C E A I I L I S F I
C N R N N R E T R Z G I A W K
R O G G T I S I Z T N E R G S
Z M M A N S N U I G I I C N A
E L E R S I P E N G T K I I S
W H D O G I D I D I N D N L T
T A R I R S N A N R I I E I N
E C I S I A N G E M A T M A R
C S V G N I E N S R P G A S N
```

CINEMA

CROSS-STITCH

DANCE

GARDENING

GOLF

KNITTING

PAINTING

PUZZLES

READING

SAILING

SKIING

SWIMMING

THEATRE

TRAVEL

WATCHING TV

WRITING

Boxing Away

Fit all the listed words into the grid, crossword-style.

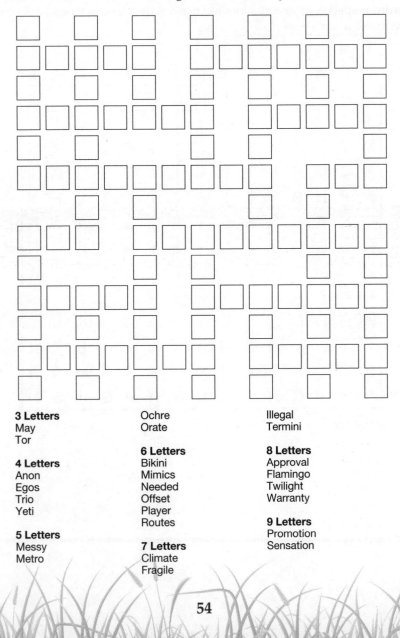

3 Letters
May
Tor

4 Letters
Anon
Egos
Trio
Yeti

5 Letters
Messy
Metro

Ochre
Orate

6 Letters
Bikini
Mimics
Needed
Offset
Player
Routes

7 Letters
Climate
Fragile

Illegal
Termini

8 Letters
Approval
Flamingo
Twilight
Warranty

9 Letters
Promotion
Sensation

Word Sliders

How many five-letter words can you spell out using the sliders? One word is spelled out for you already. Each slider can be slid up or down to reveal a single letter.

Up and Down

This pattern appears almost to be three-dimensional, and if you view it from a short distance it even seems to be moving. Colour it in to bring it even more to life!

Touchy Letters

Place one letter from A to F into every empty box, so that each row and column contains all six different letters. Also, identical letters can't be in touching boxes – not even diagonally.

F					A
	C			B	
		B	F		
		C	E		
	E			F	
A					C

Minesweeper

Can you work out where the hidden mines are? Some of the empty squares contain mines – mark them in. Clues in some squares show the number of mines in touching squares, including diagonally touching squares. No more than one mine may be placed per square.

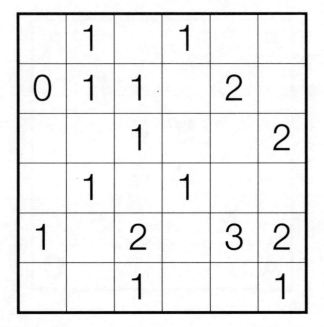

Order Recall

First, cover up the bottom of the page (below the dividing line), then spend up to a minute remembering the order of the list of countries below, then cover it over, wait a few seconds, and then see if you can recall the order that the countries were in. You'll be given the list again.

1. Ireland	6. Finland	11. Bermuda
2. France	7. Australia	12. Bhutan
3. Denmark	8. Austria	13. Fiji
4. Norway	9. Sudan	14. Greece
5. Egypt	10. Belarus	15. Germany

Australia	Austria	Belarus	Bermuda
Bhutan	Denmark	Egypt	Fiji
Finland	France	Germany	Greece
Ireland	Norway	Sudan	

_____ _____ _____

_____ _____ _____

_____ _____ _____

_____ _____ _____

_____ _____ _____

Missing Details

Using your imagination, can you use a pen or pencil to convert these squares into pictures of four different **gifts you might give to friends**? For example, one could be a photo frame, and another a jewellery box.

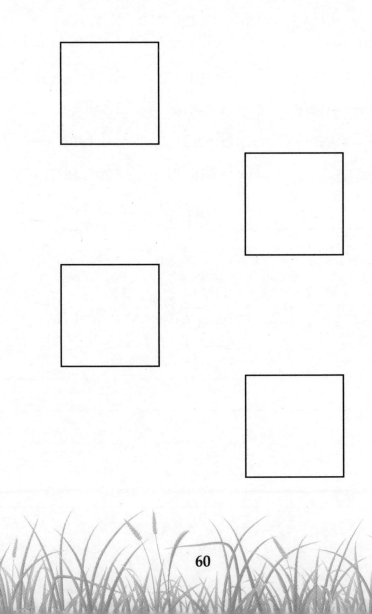

Deleted Letters

Delete one letter from each pair of letters to reveal four hidden words. For example, CD AL TM would lead to C̶D AL T̶M̶, revealing CAT.

HP RO LR TS NE

AC LR IE VL NE RT

RB OI RN OU SR

TP IE NM AE NL YS

Word Paths

How many words of three or more letters can you find in this square? Find words by moving horizontally or vertically (but not diagonally) from letter to touching letter, and without revisiting a square in a single word. There is also one word that uses every letter.

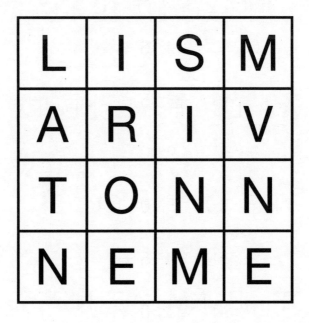

L	I	S	M
R	I	V
A	R	I	V
T	O	N	N
N	E	M	E

Fancy a challenge? If so, can you find 25 words?

Time Totals

Exercise your mind with these time calculations. Just add the two times, or subtract the second time from the first as appropriate.

19:45 - 15:40 = | : |

03:15 - 00:15 = | : |

11:45 - 06:05 = | : |

08:30 + 09:00 = | : |

11:25 + 08:10 = | : |

23:20 - 08:15 = | : |

10:30 - 06:50 = | : |

04:00 + 09:35 = | : |

23:20 - 12:15 = | : |

01:30 + 01:30 = | : |

A Quieter Sound

Can you transform LOUD into PURR in just five steps? At each step you should change a single letter to form a new word, but without rearranging the order of any of the letters. For example, you could start by stepping from LOUD to LAUD, and then from LAUD to LARD.

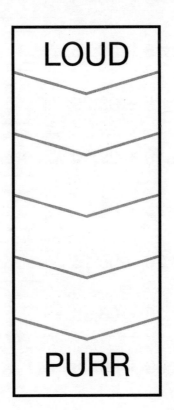

Rhyming Lines

See if you can come up with a rhyming second line for each of these extremely brief poems – the more ridiculous the better!

I sat and watched the world go by,

_____

One day I went out for a walk,

_____

A lonely fox came up to say,

_____

Colouring Therapy

The foreground circles seem almost to float on top of this pattern.
Colour it in and see if the effect remains!

Letter Circle

How many words of three or more letters can you find in this letter circle? Each word should use the centre letter plus two or more of the other letters, and no letter can be used more than once in a single word. There is one word that uses every letter.

Fancy a challenge? If so, can you find 35 words?

Missing Signs

Give your mind a workout by writing the missing mathematical sign into each of these equations: +, −, × or ÷.

40 ☐ 8 = 5   55 ☐ 6 = 49

66 ☐ 11 = 6   44 ☐ 10 = 34

12 ☐ 9 = 108   3 ☐ 10 = 30

121 ☐ 11 = 11   36 ☐ 13 = 49

27 ☐ 13 = 14   6 ☐ 10 = 60

9 ☐ 3 = 27   5 ☐ 5 = 1

5 ☐ 10 = 50   60 ☐ 10 = 50

11 ☐ 65 = 76   15 ☐ 1 = 16

4 ☐ 9 = 36   10 ☐ 12 = 120

3 ☐ 3 = 9   12 ☐ 12 = 1

Word Fit

Fit all the listed words into the grid, crossword-style.

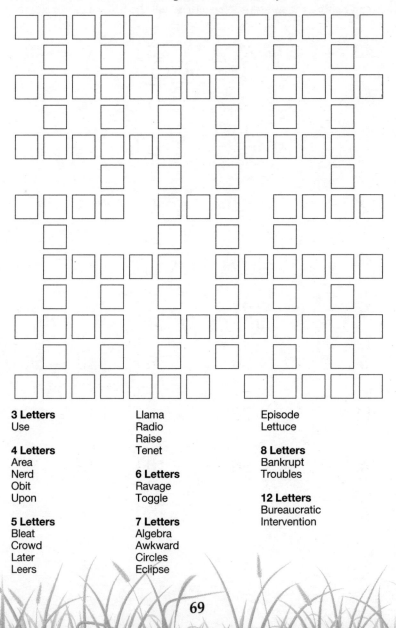

3 Letters
Use

4 Letters
Area
Nerd
Obit
Upon

5 Letters
Bleat
Crowd
Later
Leers

Llama
Radio
Raise
Tenet

6 Letters
Ravage
Toggle

7 Letters
Algebra
Awkward
Circles
Eclipse

Episode
Lettuce

8 Letters
Bankrupt
Troubles

12 Letters
Bureaucratic
Intervention

Every Other Letter

In the following list of vegetables, every other letter has been removed. Can you restore the missing letters to reveal the full set of vegetables?

B_E_R_O_

_U_H_O_M

_O_A_O

_A_B_G_

C_C_M_E_

Hourglass Maze

Can you find your way through this hourglass-shaped maze, travelling from the entrance at the top all the way down to the exit at the bottom?

Mini Crossword

Solve each of the clues to complete this mini-crossword grid.

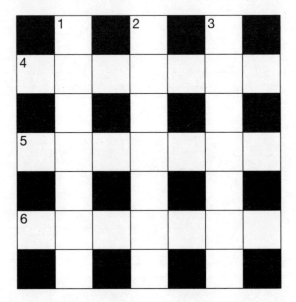

Across
4 Book-lending location (7)
5 Omitted (7)
6 Initial movement resistance (7)

Down
1 Becomes ill (7)
2 Get ready (7)
3 Giveaway (7)

The Mindfulness Puzzle Book

Mental Maths

Massage your brain with these maths calculations – do as many as you can without using a calculator or making written notes.

116 ÷ 2 = ☐   12 × 13 = ☐

64 - 5 = ☐   45 - 27 = ☐

13 + 39 = ☐   12 ÷ 6 = ☐

44 - 11 = ☐   2 × 5 = ☐

21 - 6 = ☐   54 - 19 = ☐

9 + 32 = ☐   21 + 38 = ☐

6 + 31 = ☐   47 - 8 = ☐

30 + 13 = ☐   5 × 16 = ☐

8 × 17 = ☐   45 - 6 = ☐

95 - 27 = ☐   12 × 4 = ☐

Rectangles and Squares

Draw along some of the dashed lines to divide the grid into a set of rectangles and squares, so that every rectangle or square contains exactly one number. That number must always be equal to the number of grid squares within the rectangle or square.

Link Words

Find a common English word to place in each gap, so that both when attached to the end of the first word and when attached to the start of the second word you end up with two more English words. For example, **birth _ _ _ break** could be solved using **day**, making **birthday** and **daybreak**.

child   _ _ _ _   wink

idea   _ _ _ _   less

tread   _ _ _ _   ion

Family Pets

Can you find all of the listed animals in the grid? They are written forwards or backwards in any direction, including diagonally.

```
A S M B T H T E T L A T P K U
D H T A S R S T T E I R S O E
U O R O A I A I O S S B O I P
C R T O O F B G E R O U R R R
K S T T D B G A I R R A O E A
O E R L A K R B C R E A G M G
N O L R C T H G S H E D P S U
T H S I F D L O G Y B G U N O
R O R E T S M A H G N E D I S
S R I T R O G O D A F O B U S
R G I P A E N I U G C T P I B
O R N E R P S C H I C K E N E
R A D N I G G L R A E E A I A
G E O I N D R D T G R S C K G
A U L C O C K A T I E L A O E
```

BUDGERIGAR
CAT
CHICKEN
COCKATIEL
DOG
DUCK
GERBIL
GOLDFISH

GUINEA PIG
HAMSTER
HORSE
MOUSE
PARROT
PONY
RABBIT
TORTOISE

Brain Chains

Can you solve each of the three brain chains completely in your head, without making any written notes? Start with the bold number at the top, and then apply each maths operation in turn. Write your final result in at the bottom.

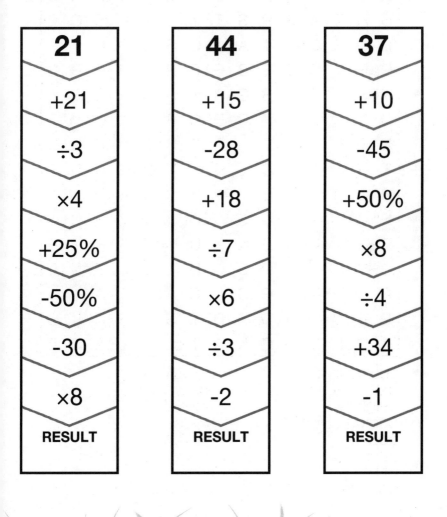

21	44	37
+21	+15	+10
÷3	-28	-45
×4	+18	+50%
+25%	÷7	×8
-50%	×6	÷4
-30	÷3	+34
×8	-2	-1
RESULT	RESULT	RESULT

Arrow Word

All of this crossword's clues are given inside the grid.

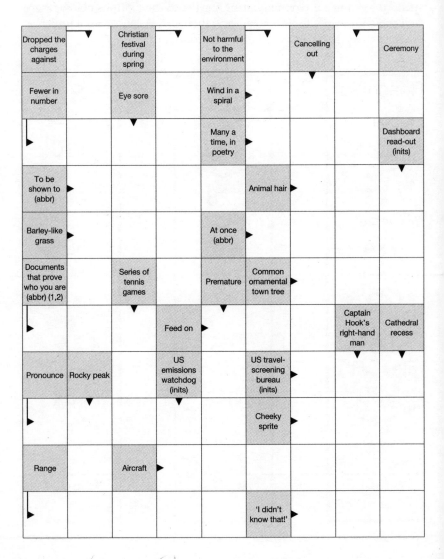

Missing Items

First, cover up the bottom of the page (below the dividing line), then spend up to a minute remembering the list of beach items below, then cover it over, wait a few seconds, and then see if you can spot which ones are missing from the list at the bottom of the page.

Beach ball	Kite	Recliner
Rubber ring	Sandcastle	Spade
Seashell	Windbreak	Parasol
Pebble	Noodle	Flippers
Bucket	Goggles	Towel

Bucket	Flippers	Goggles
Kite	Parasol	Pebble
Seashell	Spade	Windbreak

_____ _____ _____

_____ _____ _____

Flying Around

Rearrange each set of boxes to spell out a series of words that you would associate with an airport.

Puzzle 1

E	DE	RT	PA	UR

Puzzle 2

TS	S	OR	SP	PA

Puzzle 3

NE	TI	AR	AN	QU

Puzzle 4

NT	EME	UNC	NO	AN

Alternating Arcs

If you colour in the curvier shapes in a darker colour than the straighter shapes, this image may appear to have some gentle movement as you look at it!

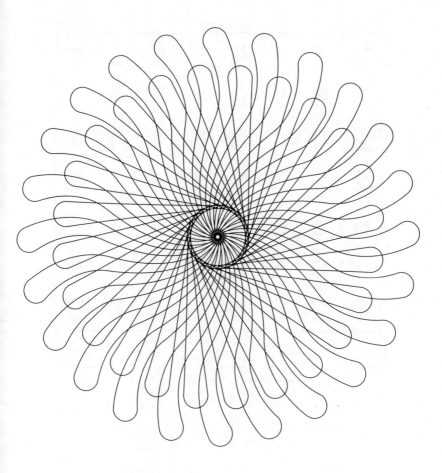

Domino Set

Draw solid lines to divide the grid into a full set of standard dominoes, with exactly one of each domino. A '0' represents a blank on a traditional domino. Use the check-off chart to help you keep track of which dominoes you've placed.

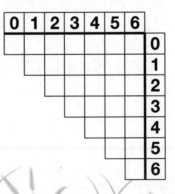

3	4	4	0	5	0	5	6
2	6	5	0	1	3	4	1
2	0	4	3	6	1	4	1
2	1	3	3	1	4	5	2
6	5	6	4	1	4	2	5
1	0	3	2	2	0	0	5
6	2	6	6	3	5	0	3

0	1	2	3	4	5	6	
							0
							1
							2
							3
							4
							5
							6

Animal Anagrams

Each of the following phrases can be rearranged to form the name of an animal. Can you solve them all?

A RA JUG

MESH ART

POET LANE

I AM DOLLAR

I SCORN HERO

Missing Vowels

All of the vowels have been deleted from the following words. Can you restore them by working out what the original words were?

TVT

VTV

BV

VB

DDD

Lower the Pace

Can you transform FAST into HERE in just five steps? At each step you should change a single letter to form a new word, but without rearranging the order of any of the letters. For example, you could start by stepping from FAST to PAST, and then from PAST to PASS.

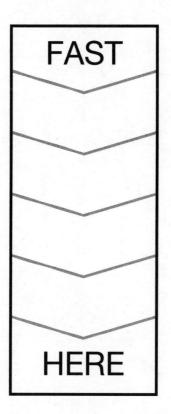

FAST

HERE

On Reflection

Reflect each half of this image onto the other half to reveal a simple picture. The reflection should be drawn with respect to the dashed-line 'mirror'.

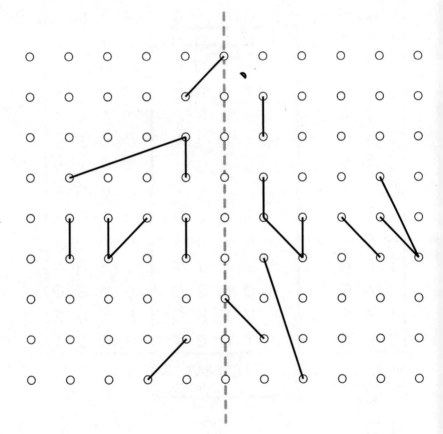

Colourful Wordsearch

Can you find all of the listed words in the grid? Words are written forwards or backwards in any direction, including diagonally.

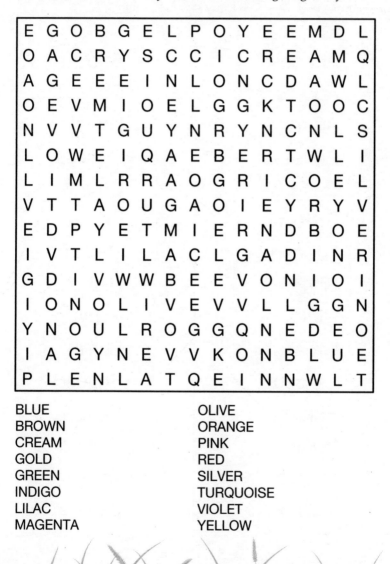

E	G	O	B	G	E	L	P	O	Y	E	E	M	D	L
O	A	C	R	Y	S	C	C	I	C	R	E	A	M	Q
A	G	E	E	E	I	N	L	O	N	C	D	A	W	L
O	E	V	M	I	O	E	L	G	G	K	T	O	O	C
N	V	V	T	G	U	Y	N	R	Y	N	C	N	L	S
L	O	W	E	I	Q	A	E	B	E	R	T	W	L	I
L	I	M	L	R	R	A	O	G	R	I	C	O	E	L
V	T	T	A	O	U	G	A	O	I	E	Y	R	Y	V
E	D	P	Y	E	T	M	I	E	R	N	D	B	O	E
I	V	T	L	I	L	A	C	L	G	A	D	I	N	R
G	D	I	V	W	W	B	E	E	V	O	N	I	O	I
I	O	N	O	L	I	V	E	V	V	L	L	G	G	N
Y	N	O	U	L	R	O	G	G	Q	N	E	D	E	O
I	A	G	Y	N	E	V	V	K	O	N	B	L	U	E
P	L	E	N	L	A	T	Q	E	I	N	N	W	L	T

BLUE
BROWN
CREAM
GOLD
GREEN
INDIGO
LILAC
MAGENTA

OLIVE
ORANGE
PINK
RED
SILVER
TURQUOISE
VIOLET
YELLOW

Anagram Pairs

Draw lines to join each word in the left-hand column to a word in the right-hand column, where the two words are anagrams of one another. For example, you could join MELONS to LEMONS.

Abodes	Adobes
Adores	Debugs
Allure	Laurel
Bosses	Obsess
Budges	Organs
Creams	Prince
Dashed	Report
Filter	Rights
Girths	Scream
Groans	Sealed
Leased	Shaded
Pincer	Simper
Porter	Soared
Primes	Trifle
Rushes	Ushers

Word Paths

How many words of three or more letters can you find in this square?
Find words by moving horizontally or vertically (but not diagonally)
from letter to touching letter, and without revisiting a square in a
single word. There is also one word that uses every letter.

S	T	R	E
C	S	I	S
H	L	M	S
O	O	S	E

Fancy a challenge? If so, can you find 30 words?

The Numbers Game

Can you form each of the three totals below, using all of the listed numbers just once each? For example, you could form a total of 25 by adding the 6 and 4, multiplying by 2, and then adding the remaining 5.

$$2 \qquad 4 \qquad 5 \qquad 6$$

Totals:

21

31

41

Reverse Words

Can you solve each of the following clues? Each pair of clues reveal the same word, except that the solution to each 'b' clue is the **reverse** of the 'a' clue. For example, if the 'a' solution is DOG then the 'b' solution will be GOD, and vice versa.

Puzzle 1
a. Wild relation of the dog
b. A steady or continuous stream of liquid

Puzzle 2
a. To create another way, if you're an artist
b. A prison guard

Puzzle 3
a. To bring a parcel to its destination
b. Thoroughly disliked

Puzzle 4
a. Removes the skin from fruit
b. Dreaming state

Image Combination

Imagine combining these two images, so each white square in one is filled with the contents of the corresponding square in the other image. How many stars would there be in total?

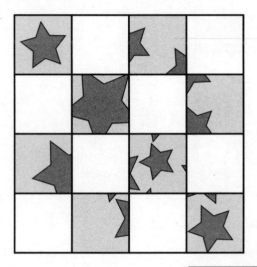

Mini Crossword

Solve each of the clues to complete this mini-crossword grid.

Across
1 Amount consumed (6)
4 On one's own (5)
6 Circumvent (5)
8 Fire-breathing beast (6)

Down
1 Diseased (3)
2 Sports stadium (5)
3 Delete (5)
4 Enquired (5)
5 Theatre show with sung music (5)
7 Lair (3)

Impossible Colours

Colour in this image as you think appropriate – but no matter how you do it, the resulting picture will still form an impossible triangle of cubes!

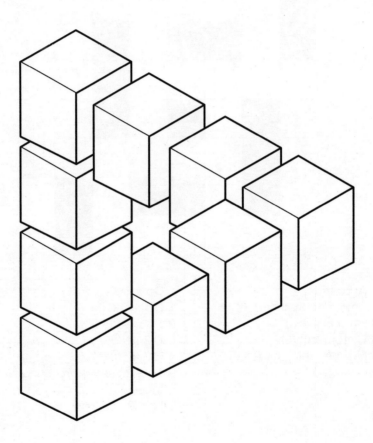

Cave Maze

Can you find your way through this maze, travelling from the entrance at the top all the way down to the exit at the bottom? The maze contains some larger cave rooms, which you can pass through in just the same way as you would travel along any corridor.

Word Placement

Fit all the listed words into the grid, crossword-style.

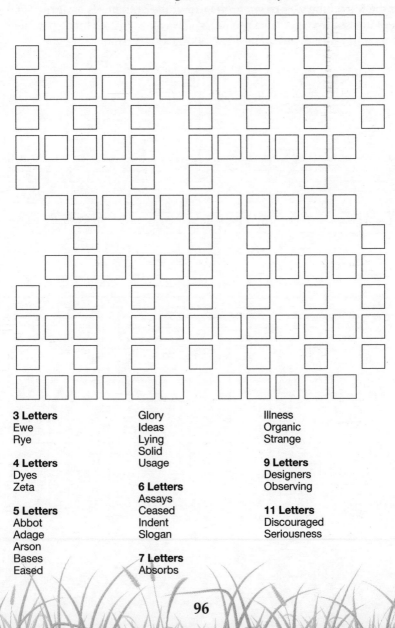

3 Letters
Ewe
Rye

4 Letters
Dyes
Zeta

5 Letters
Abbot
Adage
Arson
Bases
Eased

Glory
Ideas
Lying
Solid
Usage

6 Letters
Assays
Ceased
Indent
Slogan

7 Letters
Absorbs

Illness
Organic
Strange

9 Letters
Designers
Observing

11 Letters
Discouraged
Seriousness

Spot the Changes

First, cover up the bottom of the page (below the dividing line), then spend up to a minute remembering the list of things you might want to pack to take on a trip below, then cover it over, wait a few seconds, and then see if you can spot which ones have been replaced on the copy of the list at the bottom of the page.

Suitcase	Passport	Credit card
Sunglasses	Hotel booking	Currency
Sun block	Boarding pass	Wallet
Train ticket	Clothes	Toiletries
Shoes	Driving licence	Watch

Briefcase	Passport	Credit card
Sun hat	Motel booking	Currency
Moisturizer	Boarding pass	Comb
Car park ticket	Clothes	Toiletries
Shoes	Driving glasses	Watch

Dot Drawing

Try this creative task by drawing straight lines to join some, or all, of the dots together. See if you can come up with a pattern or picture, even with this restricted set of dots! Even if you have no idea what you want to draw, just start by joining dots at random and see what it begins to look like!

Arrow Word

All of this crossword's clues are given inside the grid.

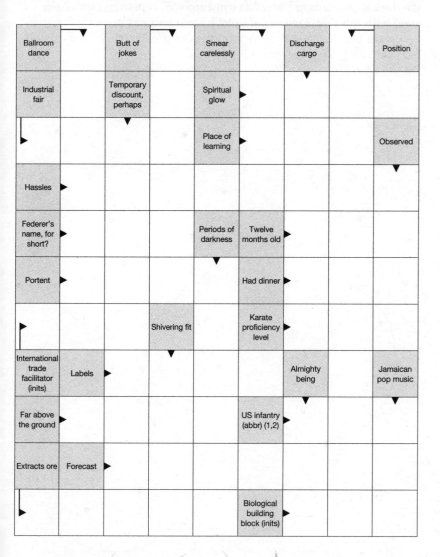

Missing Details

Using your imagination, can you use a pen or pencil to convert these circles into pictures of four different **foods**? For example, one could be a pizza, and another could be an orange cut in half.

Link Words

Find a common English word to place in each gap, so that both when attached to the end of the first word and when attached to the start of the second word you end up with two more English words. For example, **birth _ _ _ break** could be solved using **day**, making **birthday** and **daybreak**.

honey _ _ _ _ light

over _ _ _ _ _ walk

fire _ _ _ _ _ hop

Flower Power

Can you find the pair of identical flowers? The remaining five illustrations each have slight differences from one another. The illustrations are rotated in order to provide a tougher challenge!

Letter Circle

How many words of three or more letters can you find in this letter circle? Each word should use the centre letter plus two or more of the other letters, and no letter can be used more than once in a single word. There is one word that uses every letter.

Fancy a challenge? If so, can you find 40 words?

Missing Signs

Give your mind a workout by writing the missing mathematical sign into each of these equations: +, −, × or ÷.

43 $\boxed{}$ 4 = 47   16 $\boxed{}$ 4 = 12

6 $\boxed{}$ 40 = 46   6 $\boxed{}$ 12 = 72

72 $\boxed{}$ 8 = 9   78 $\boxed{}$ 7 = 85

57 $\boxed{}$ 2 = 59   20 $\boxed{}$ 10 = 30

12 $\boxed{}$ 12 = 1   30 $\boxed{}$ 13 = 17

56 $\boxed{}$ 16 = 40   12 $\boxed{}$ 19 = 31

2 $\boxed{}$ 16 = 18   6 $\boxed{}$ 3 = 18

4 $\boxed{}$ 8 = 32   88 $\boxed{}$ 8 = 11

5 $\boxed{}$ 10 = 50   10 $\boxed{}$ 6 = 60

5 $\boxed{}$ 34 = 39   16 $\boxed{}$ 64 = 80

Start and End

For each of these puzzles, add the same letter to both the start and end of the given fragment to form a normal English word. For example, add S to _TART_ to form STARTS.

TYLU

ALLO

OPKNO

EWTO

ECU

EFUSE

IXE

Mnemonic Memory

Using an acronym as a memory aid can really help with remembering a list of items. See if you can use the fruit acronyms on this page, in the first letter of each column, to help you remember each of the words. Use the empty lists at the bottom of the page to see how you get on.

Article	**L**ove	**G**ame
Periodical	**E**njoyment	**R**ecreation
Publication	**M**indfulness	**A**ctivity
Letters	**O**bliging	**P**ractice
Essay	**N**iceness	**E**xercise

_____   _____   _____

_____   _____   _____

_____   _____   _____

_____   _____   _____

_____   _____   _____

Painting Materials

Can you find all of the listed painting materials in the grid? They are written forwards or backwards in any direction, including diagonally.

```
I  R  S  U  S  A  N  O  Y  A  R  C  A  A  E
R  G  R  S  T  N  I  A  P  L  I  O  C  N  P
W  S  S  T  Y  C  S  T  B  R  L  R  S  T  E
O  A  R  S  A  L  C  I  R  R  Y  S  A  R  S
N  S  T  O  P  H  C  C  L  U  A  I  I  T
S  T  E  E  A  I  T  B  I  R  T  S  F  S  S
L  R  C  L  R  I  T  C  S  S  C  S  H  A  L
E  C  K  P  Y  C  P  T  N  L  S  L  A  E  A
T  P  R  A  R  A  O  E  L  A  I  I  N  L  S
S  S  L  C  I  C  P  L  V  E  P  C  H  R  I
A  C  A  N  C  E  E  N  O  O  F  N  P  Y  G
P  T  T  R  E  S  A  R  E  U  O  E  T  G  S
L  S  T  B  E  C  O  R  E  P  R  P  I  L  P
L  L  S  T  C  S  E  A  R  C  O  S  S  U  T
S  P  A  P  E  R  O  P  A  L  E  T  T  E  E
```

ACRYLIC PAINTS
BRUSHES
CANVAS
CHALK
CLAY
CRAYON
ERASER
FELT-TIPS

GLUE
OIL PAINTS
PALETTE
PAPER
PASTELS
PENCILS
PENS
WATERCOLOURS

Colour-in Contrast

If you colour this image in with contrasting colours in a chequerboard pattern, you might find it rather hard to look at!

Simple Sudoku

See how quickly you can complete these easy puzzles – just place the digits from 1 to 4 into every row, column and 2×2 box for each puzzle.

Puzzle 1

		4	
		2	
	3		
	4		

Puzzle 2

		1	2
3	1		

Puzzle 3

	2		
	1		
		1	
		4	

Puzzle 4

		3		1
4		1		

Brain Chains

Can you solve each of the three brain chains completely in your head, without making any written notes? Start with the bold number at the top, and then apply each maths operation in turn. Write your final result in at the bottom.

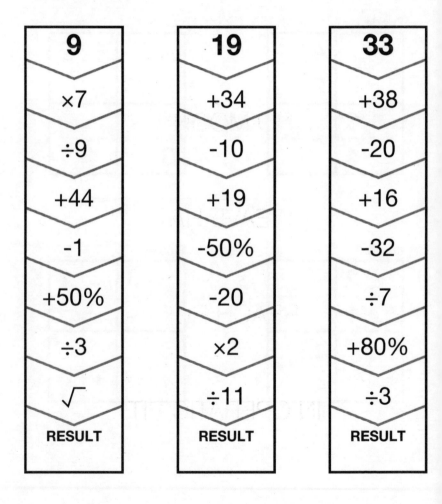

9	19	33
×7	+34	+38
÷9	-10	-20
+44	+19	+16
-1	-50%	-32
+50%	-20	÷7
÷3	×2	+80%
√	÷11	÷3
RESULT	RESULT	RESULT

Weather Words

Each of the following phrases can be rearranged to form a word connected to the weather. Can you solve them all?

NO CYCLE

NO MOONS

WEAVE HAT

REACH RUIN

IN OPERATIC PIT

Join the Dots

Join each of these dots in increasing numerical order, starting from 1, to reveal something you might see on holiday.

No Repeats

Can you write a number from 1 to 7 in each empty square, so that
every row and column of the grid contains each number exactly once?

7		4		6		3
	6				4	
2			6			1
		7	5	1		
1			4			7
	1				6	
6		1		5		2

Missing Vowels

All of the vowels have been deleted from the following words. Can you restore them by working out what the original words were?

MXMM

TLVSN

QTRL

CBC

PPRL

Word Depository

Fit all the listed words into the grid, crossword-style.

3 Letters
Eel
Ten

4 Letters
Elan
Espy
Icon
Wrap

5 Letters
Apron
Lilac

Plugs
Ruler

6 Letters
Expand
Lyrics
Pepper
Upkeep

7 Letters
Connect
Declare
Emperor
Sockets

8 Letters
Cultural
Esoteric
Landlord
Recalled

9 Letters
Presently
Wallpaper

11 Letters
Stereotyped

Memory List

It's a good mindfulness technique to make a list of all the things you need to remember, so you don't worry about forgetting them. But this doesn't mean you should never exercise your memory!

Spend up to a minute remembering the list of names below, then cover it over, wait a few seconds, and then see how many you can write out again in the gaps at the bottom of the page.

Lewis	Sara	Aarti
Joey	Arvind	Matthew
John	Owen	Sunil
Daniel	Gayatri	Tatiana

_____   _____   _____

_____   _____   _____

_____   _____   _____

_____   _____   _____

Mental Maths

Massage your brain with these maths calculations – do as many as you can without using a calculator or making written notes.

17 + 79 =

28 + 32 =

5 × 10 =

14 × 3 =

25 + 18 =

5 × 16 =

56 - 9 =

31 + 12 =

27 + 10 =

6 × 4 =

87 - 23 =

29 - 21 =

43 - 25 =

17 × 6 =

11 × 15 =

5 × 7 =

12 × 15 =

10 × 4 =

73 - 6 =

172 ÷ 4 =

Arrow Word

All of this crossword's clues are given inside the grid.

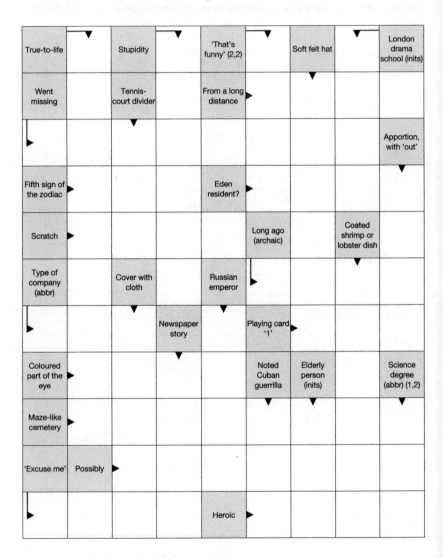

Every Other Letter

In the following list of vegetables, every other letter has been removed. Can you restore the missing letters to reveal the full set of vegetables?

L_T_U_E

_A_R_T

A_T_C_O_E

_A_S_I_

_R_C_O_I

Letter Circle

How many words of three or more letters can you find in this letter circle? Each word should use the centre letter plus two or more of the other letters, and no letter can be used more than once in a single word. There is one word that uses every letter.

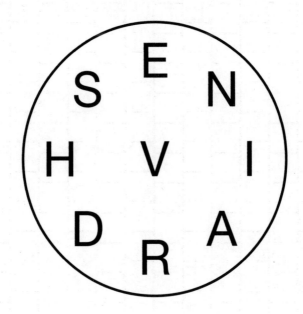

Fancy a challenge? If so, can you find 75 words?

Sliding Squares

Colour these squares in using an alternating pattern and you might find that they appear to start sliding around the page!

Ordered Recall

First, cover up the bottom of the page (below the dividing line), then spend up to a minute remembering the order of the list of colours below, then cover it over, wait a few seconds, and then see if you can recall the order that the colours were in. You'll be given the list again.

1. Auburn
2. Emerald
3. Blue
4. Green
5. Pink
6. Purple
7. Magenta
8. Cyan
9. White
10. Black
11. Fuchsia
12. Brown
13. Yellow
14. Grey
15. Azure

Auburn
Brown
Green
Purple

Azure
Cyan
Grey
White

Black
Emerald
Magenta
Yellow

Blue
Fuchsia
Pink

A Circular Route

Can you find your way through this circular maze, travelling from the entrance at the top all the way down to the exit at the bottom?

Minesweeper

Can you work out where the hidden mines are? Some of the empty squares contain mines – mark them in. Clues in some squares show the number of mines in touching squares, including diagonally touching squares. No more than one mine may be placed per square.

	1				1
2		2		3	
	3		2		2
		2	4		4
	2		3		
				2	

Deleted Pairs

Delete one letter from each pair of letters to reveal four hidden words.
For example, CD AL TM would lead to C~~D~~ A~~L~~ T~~M~~, revealing CAT.

IO NM EA LG OI NM ES

NM EI NL GD FE IU TL

DS MR EI AL ET

GF RI NA IN SD HY

Mini Crossword

Solve each of the clues to complete this mini-crossword grid.

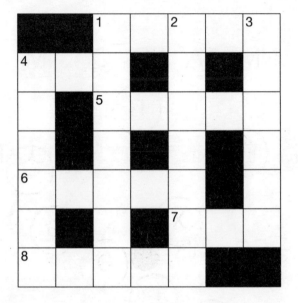

Across
1 The Paris underground (5)
4 Tea, for the pretentious (3)
5 Connects (5)
6 Welsh breed of dog (5)
7 Convulsive muscle twitch (3)
8 Prepared (5)

Down
1 Mediterranean island (7)
2 Threefoldness (7)
3 In the hope of being paid (2,4)
4 Be of the same opinion (6)

Word Orbit

By picking one letter from each orbit in turn, working in from the outermost ring to the innermost ring, how many four-letter words can you find?

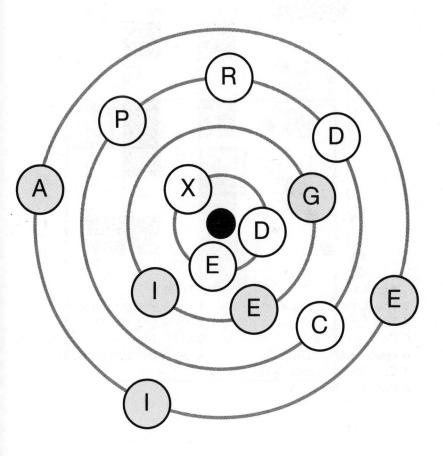

Find the Path

Join some of the dots with horizontal and vertical lines to form a single path. The path should not touch or cross either itself or any of the solid blocks. Numbers outside the grid specify the exact number of dots in their row or column that are visited by the path. The start and end of the path are given to you, and are marked by the solid dots.

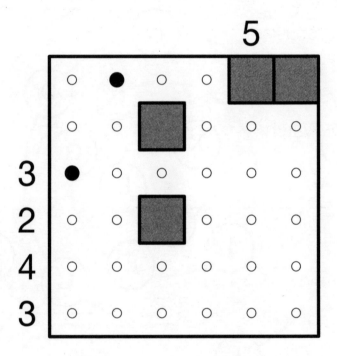

Rhyming Lines

See if you can come up with a rhyming second line for each of these extremely brief poems – the more ridiculous the better!

I sit beneath this walnut tree,

_____

Upon the lake I saw one day,

_____

The hourly news was on the box,

_____

Birds Around

Each of the following phrases can be rearranged to form the name of a bird. Can you solve them all?

NO CALF

OR WARPS

LUG SEAL

BALD BRICK

DO KEEP CROW

Just for Fun

See if you can come up with an amusing or witty conclusion to each of these partial jokes! There are no correct answers here – the idea is just to provide a bit of creative relaxation.

What do you get if you add a packet of crisps to a pot of tea?

_____

Did you hear the one about the cow that walked into the bar?

_____

Two geese take a visit to the supermarket. One goose says to the other:

"_____"

Visit to the Beach

Can you find all of the listed entries in the grid? They are written forwards or backwards in any direction, including diagonally.

```
L G S S S K A L B G M C K U A
I U L W R S S I L R B W R B S
N K R I S G L I C E C R E A M
I M H M R L N N T G K E V T A
H N H M E O L I M A L R T H T
H I E I N L K E R A A L O I T
K S I N I S T S H R H B B N S
S U N G L A S S E S E E I G S
E N R C C L T N A V A B S T B
M S S L E W O T H C A E B R S
B H M E R E M I H R D W S U E
V I E E T I A B I K I N I N R
R N R K L I A S A E R W A K R
H E B A L L E R B M U N U S S
D A I B L L S R N S O N I R H
```

BATHING TRUNKS
BEACH BALL
BEACH TOWEL
BIKINI
ICE CREAM
KITE
RECLINER
RUBBER RING

SANDCASTLE
SEASHELLS
SNORKEL
SUNGLASSES
SUNSHINE
SUN UMBRELLA
SWIMMING
WAVES

Mental Maths

Massage your brain with these maths calculations – do as many as you can without using a calculator or making written notes.

$10 \times 7 =$ ⬚ $25 + 82 =$ ⬚

$135 \div 5 =$ ⬚ $12 \times 8 =$ ⬚

$9 \times 7 =$ ⬚ $20 + 98 =$ ⬚

$28 + 9 =$ ⬚ $65 - 16 =$ ⬚

$57 + 12 =$ ⬚ $63 - 11 =$ ⬚

$172 \div 2 =$ ⬚ $32 - 28 =$ ⬚

$26 - 20 =$ ⬚ $88 - 19 =$ ⬚

$26 + 38 =$ ⬚ $26 + 87 =$ ⬚

$87 - 6 =$ ⬚ $46 - 28 =$ ⬚

$9 \times 17 =$ ⬚ $58 + 10 =$ ⬚

Word Sliders

How many five-letter words can you spell out using the sliders? One word is spelled out for you already. Each slider can be slid up or down to reveal a single letter.

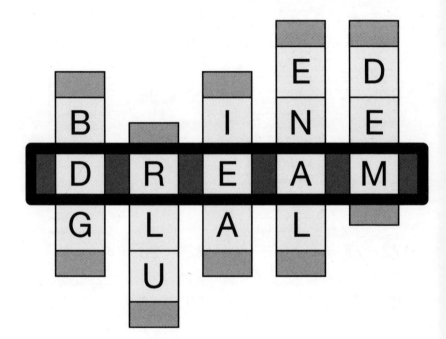

Missing Details

Using your imagination, can you use a pen or pencil to convert these bottomless triangles into pictures of four **things you might see outside**? For example, one could be a tent, and another could be the roof of a building.

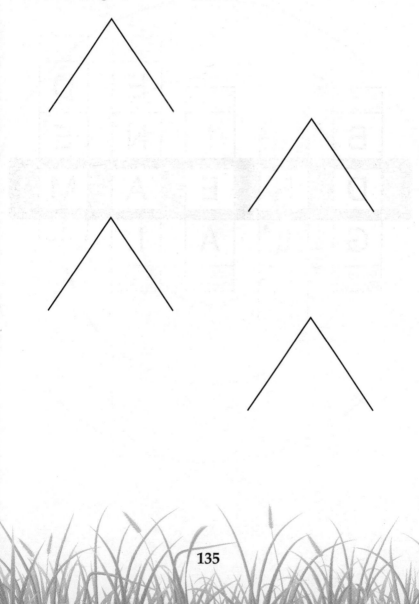

Spiral Colour

Colour this pattern in as you see fit. If you use contrasting colours, it might start to send you to sleep!

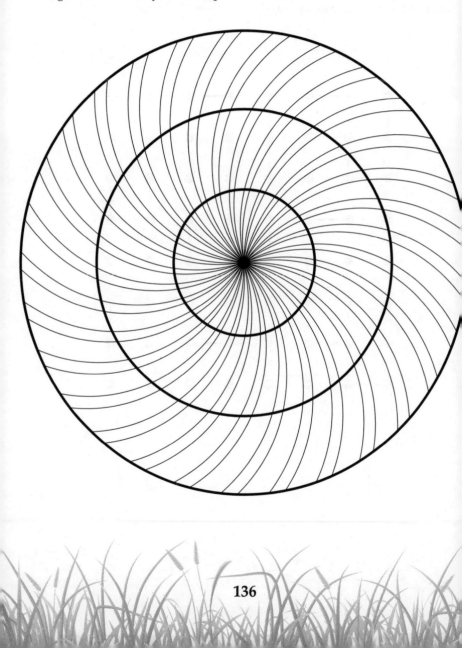

Loop the Loop

Join all of the dots using only horizontal or vertical lines to form a single loop. The loop can only visit each dot once, and it can't cross over or touch itself at any point.

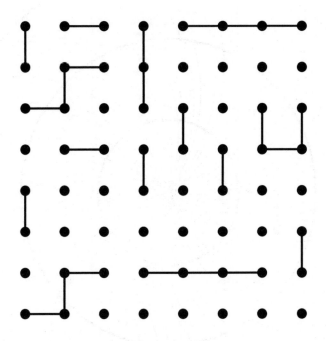

Time is Golden

Can you transform TIME into GOLD in just five steps? At each step you should change a single letter to form a new word, but without rearranging the order of any of the letters. For example, you could start by stepping from TIME to MIME, and then from MIME to MILE.

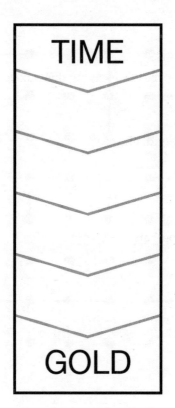

Reverse Words

Can you solve each of the following clues? Each pair of clues reveal the same word, except that the solution to each 'b' clue is the **reverse** of the 'a' clue. For example, if the 'a' solution is DOG then the 'b' solution will be GOD, and vice versa.

Puzzle 1
a. Courses served at the end of a meal
b. What you shouldn't be after solving this puzzle . . .

Puzzle 2
a. Dug out of the ground, like coal
b. Jeans material

Puzzle 3
a. A very strong smell
b. Makes a jumper, perhaps

Puzzle 4
a. Intelligent
b. Certain public transport vehicles

Classic Maze

Can you find your way through this square maze, travelling from the entrance at the top all the way down to the exit at the bottom?

Link Words

Find a common English word to place in each gap, so that both when attached to the end of the first word and when attached to the start of the second word you end up with two more English words. For example, **birth** _ _ _ **break** could be solved using **day**, making **birthday** and **daybreak**.

broad _ _ _ _ away

man _ _ _ _ _ boat

snow _ _ _ _ _ wood

Word Paths

How many words of three or more letters can you find in this square?
Find words by moving horizontally or vertically (but not diagonally)
from letter to touching letter, and without revisiting a square in a
single word. There is also one word that uses every letter.

I	B	I	S
L	I	E	N
I	T	S	O
R	E	S	P

Fancy a challenge? If so, can you find 30 words?

Grid Memory

Look at the pattern in the grid at the top-left of the page, then cover it over and see if you can accurately reproduce it in the empty grid at the top-right of the page. Then repeat with each of the other two grids.

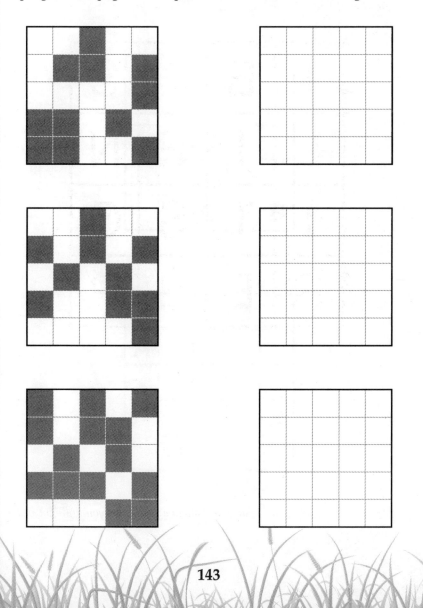

Jigsaw Letters

To solve these puzzles, place a letter from A to E into each empty square so that every row, column and bold-lined jigsaw shape contains each letter exactly once.

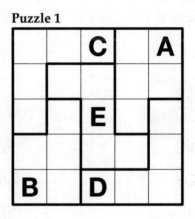

Puzzle 1

Puzzle 2

Anagram Pairs

Draw lines to join each word in the left-hand column to a word in the right-hand column, where the two words are anagrams of one another. For example, you could join MELONS to LEMONS.

Adverb	Braved
Anoint	Garden
Danger	Nation
Deeply	Piques
Equals	Remote
Equips	Sinner
Ingest	Spouse
Inners	Squeal
Meteor	Steers
Neural	Tinges
Opuses	Turner
Rawest	Unreal
Resets	Viewer
Return	Waters
Review	Yelped

Missing Symbols

Give your mind a workout by writing the missing mathematical sign into each of these equations: +, −, × or ÷.

81 ☐ 9 = 9   5 ☐ 5 = 25

20 ☐ 13 = 7   144 ☐ 12 = 12

20 ☐ 9 = 29   48 ☐ 6 = 8

35 ☐ 5 = 7   3 ☐ 21 = 24

39 ☐ 3 = 36   16 ☐ 34 = 50

3 ☐ 3 = 1   9 ☐ 7 = 63

53 ☐ 12 = 41   7 ☐ 11 = 77

2 ☐ 36 = 38   17 ☐ 19 = 36

8 ☐ 6 = 48   27 ☐ 6 = 21

56 ☐ 7 = 8   59 ☐ 12 = 47

Mini Crossword

Solve each of the clues to complete this mini-crossword grid.

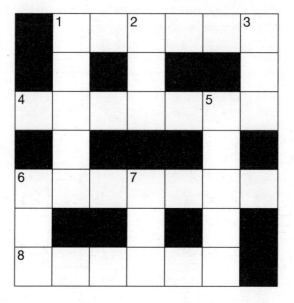

Across
1 Ordinary (6)
4 Road around the outside of a town (7)
6 The eighth planet (7)
8 Up to date (6)

Down
1 Impertinence (5)
2 Recurrent muscle-pain injury (inits) (3)
3 'Ha ha', when online (inits) (3)
5 Bother (5)
6 Tennis-court divider (3)
7 Lie in the sun, perhaps (3)

Rectangles and Squares

Draw along some of the dashed lines to divide the grid into a set of rectangles and squares, so that every rectangle or square contains exactly one number. That number must always be equal to the number of grid squares within the rectangle or square.

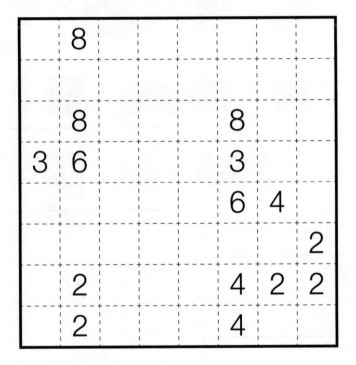

Missing Details

Using your imagination, can you use a pen or pencil to convert these pairs of parallel lines into pictures of four **everyday items**? For example, one could be an envelope and another could be a ladder.

Words Away

Fit all the listed words into the grid, crossword-style.

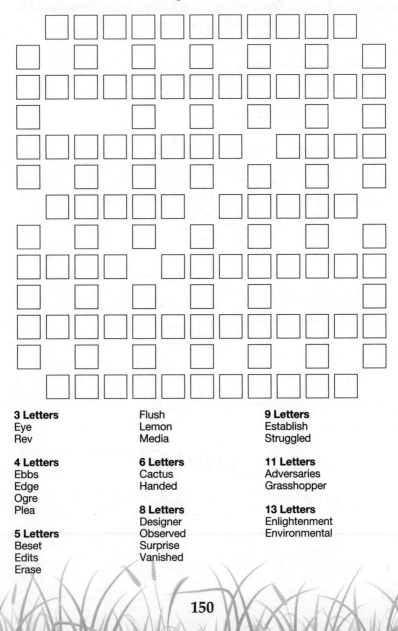

3 Letters	Flush	9 Letters
Eye	Lemon	Establish
Rev	Media	Struggled

4 Letters	6 Letters	11 Letters
Ebbs	Cactus	Adversaries
Edge	Handed	Grasshopper
Ogre		
Plea	8 Letters	13 Letters
	Designer	Enlightenment
5 Letters	Observed	Environmental
Beset	Surprise	
Edits	Vanished	
Erase		

Start and End

For each of these puzzles, add the same letter to both the start and end of the given fragment to form a normal English word. For example, add S to _TART_ to form STARTS.

OSMETI

IAMON

_UF_

YLO

AUNC

YNI

LUMN

Shape Link

Draw a series of separate paths, each connecting a pair of identical shapes. Paths only travel horizontally or vertically, and they don't cross or touch at any point. No more than one path can enter any grid square.

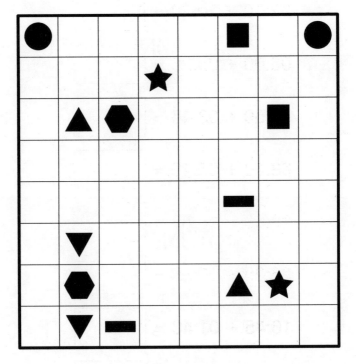

Time Totals

Exercise your mind with these time calculations. Just add the two times, or subtract the second time from the first as appropriate.

17:50 - 05:55 = [:]

22:10 - 20:20 = [:]

08:00 + 05:20 = [:]

15:50 + 03:45 = [:]

08:10 + 05:40 = [:]

18:55 - 15:55 = [:]

06:25 - 00:55 = [:]

16:45 + 01:40 = [:]

10:35 - 00:35 = [:]

13:45 - 00:25 = [:]

Touchy Letters

Place one letter from A to F into every empty box, so that each row and column contains all six different letters. Also, identical letters can't be in touching boxes – not even diagonally.

	A	D	C	F	
C					D
F					B
E					A
D					C
	B	C	D	E	

Colouring Confusion

Colour in this shape, if you can make sense of the confusing three-dimensional surfaces!

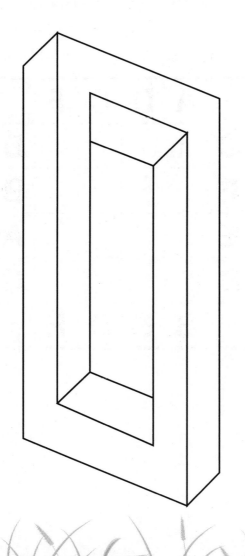

Spot the Changes

First, cover up the bottom of the page (below the dividing line), then spend up to a minute remembering the list of currencies below, then cover it over, wait a few seconds, and then see if you can spot which ones have been replaced on the copy of the list at the bottom of the page.

Dollar	Euro	Ruble
Florin	Franc	Peseta
Guilder	Złoty	Rupee
Kyat	Dram	Dirham
Yen	Baht	Rand

Dalasi	Euro	Riyal
Florin	Franc	Lek
Guilder	Złoty	Rupiah
Krona	Dram	Dinar
Yuan	Baht	Rand

Hourglass Maze

Can you find your way through this hourglass-shaped maze, travelling from the entrance at the top all the way down to the exit at the bottom?

Brain Chains

Can you solve each of the three brain chains completely in your head, without making any written notes? Start with the bold number at the top, and then apply each maths operation in turn. Write your final result in at the bottom.

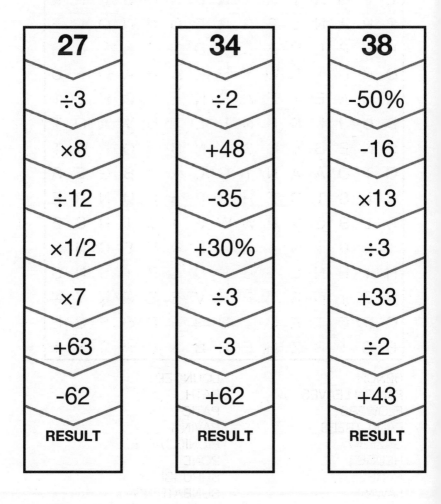

27	34	38
÷3	÷2	-50%
×8	+48	-16
÷12	-35	×13
×1/2	+30%	÷3
×7	÷3	+33
+63	-3	÷2
-62	+62	+43
RESULT	RESULT	RESULT

Relaxing in the Garden

Can you find all of the listed entries in the grid? They are written forwards or backwards in any direction, including diagonally.

```
E F G N I H T A B N U S F R P
P R A N V E G R E G N U O L F
P H P L N A O A D N O B E H R
O B D A L W Y H Z A H A O F U
N O A E T E A R N E B O H L I
D U U L R H N L E E B V A O T
O N E B L G S L N B H O R W T
G T O A A N T C E A B B G E R
N L S T R E H P P A R U N R E
S L B C V P W W E A V I R S E
I B B I N A R A B D V E C H S
H I H N E T B S C G B I S N S
H E I C R I E P V E E G N Y N
O P O I A O L B H E D G E G B
S G I P Z H E R B S S P S H I
```

BENCH
FALLEN LEAVES
FLOWERS
FRUIT TREES
GAZEBO
HEDGE
HERBS
LAWN

LOUNGER
PATH
PATIO
PAVING
PICNIC TABLE
POND
SHRUBBERY
SUNBATHING

Domino Fit

Draw solid lines to divide the grid into a full set of standard dominoes, with exactly one of each domino. A '0' represents a blank on a traditional domino. Use the check-off chart to help you keep track of which dominoes you've placed.

1	6	6	3	3	6	2	2
5	3	4	5	2	1	5	5
4	5	4	1	3	3	4	1
6	3	1	6	6	0	2	2
2	3	4	0	1	0	0	0
0	4	4	5	3	6	6	0
2	5	1	1	4	0	5	2

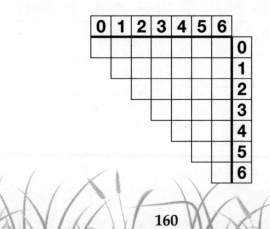

Upon Reflection

Reflect each half of this image onto the other half to reveal a simple picture. The reflection should be drawn with respect to the dashed-line 'mirror'.

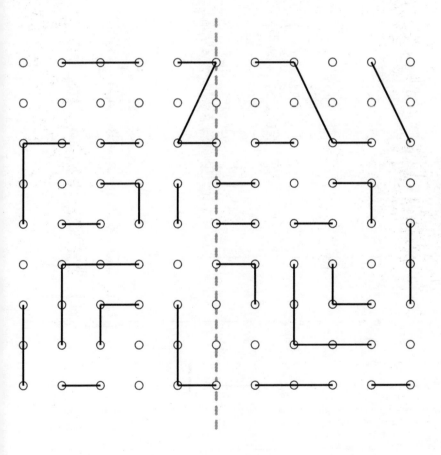

Mnemonic Memory

Using an acronym as a memory aid can really help with remembering a list of items. See if you can use the fruit acronyms on this page, in the first letter of each column, to help you remember each of the words. Use the empty lists at the bottom of the page to see how you get on.

Milk	**M**ail	**G**oogle
Eggs	**A**dvertiser	**U**ber
Loaf of bread	**N**ew Day	**A**pple
Olives	**G**uardian	**V**iacom
Nuts	**O**bserver	**A**mazon

Arrow Word

All of this crossword's clues are given inside the grid.

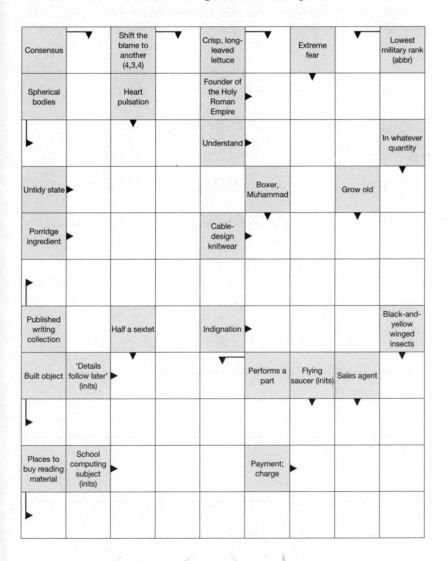

The Numbers Game

Can you form each of the three totals below, using all of the listed numbers just once each? For example, you could form a total of 37 by adding the 6 and 4, multiplying by 3, and then adding the remaining 7.

3   4   6   7

Totals:

29

59

79

The Mindfulness Puzzle Book

Tree Time

Each of the following phrases can be rearranged to form the name of a tree. Can you solve them all? Note that the name of the fifth tree consists of two words.

LIL WOW

COUNT CO

SCENT HUT

SO A MERCY

IS NOT A HUMAN

165

No Repeats

Can you write a number from 1 to 7 in each empty square, so that every row and column of the grid contains each number exactly once?

2	6				1	4
1			4			6
		6		1		
	7		1		2	
		5		2		
3			6			2
4	3				6	7

Counting Cubes

How many individual cubes have been used to build the structure below? You should assume that all 'hidden' cubes are present, and that it started off as a perfect 5×4×4 arrangement of cubes (as shown to the right) before any cubes were removed. There are no floating cubes.

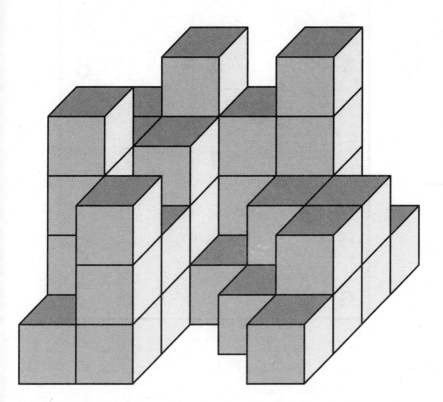

Cave Maze

Can you find your way through this maze, travelling from the entrance at the top all the way down to the exit at the bottom? The maze contains some larger cave rooms, which you can pass through in just the same way as you would travel along any corridor.

The Last Puzzle

Can you transform LAST into WORD in just five steps? At each step you should change a single letter to form a new word, but without rearranging the order of any of the letters. For example, you could start by stepping from LAST to PAST, and then from PAST to POST.

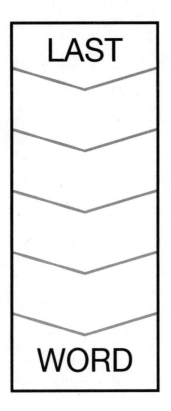

Solutions

Page 9

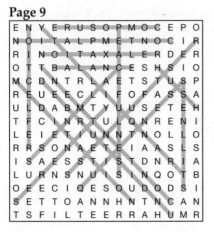

```
E N Y E R U S O P M O C E P O
N O I T A L P M E T N O C I R
R I N O I T A X A L E R D E R
O T T B A L A N C E S H S I O
M C D N T R L A E T S T U S P
R E U E E C L I F O F A S S A
U L D A B M T Y U U S E T E H
T F C I N R T U L Q N R E N I
L E I E T I U N N T N O L L O
R R S O N A E T E I A A S L S
I S A E S S T I S T D N R I A
L U R N S N U I S I N Q O T B
O E E C I Q E S O U D O D S I
S E T T O A N N H N T N C A N
T S F I L T E E R R A H U M R
```

Page 10

Accomplished, concluded, finalized, achieved

Page 11

Page 12

MESS › MASS › PASS › PALS › PALM › CALM

Page 13

2	4	1	3		1	2	4	3		3	2	4	1		4	2	1	3
1	3	4	2		3	4	2	1		4	1	2	3		1	3	2	4
3	1	2	4		4	3	1	2		1	4	3	2		2	4	3	1
4	2	3	1		2	1	3	4		2	3	1	4		3	1	4	2

Page 14

Archery, badminton, gymnastics, orienteering, trampolining

Page 15

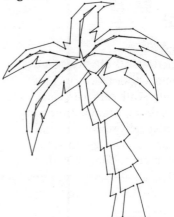

Page 16

```
    F R E E I N G    E M U S
C   O   N   O        O   T
H O W E V E R    T E N S E
O   A   I    M   E   A   W
I N N E R    A D M I R E
C   O   L    P   C   V
E R R A N T    T E C H N O
S   E   M    E   R       L
    S T R E S S    A S S E T
S   R   N    S   T   K   A
A G E N T    A M U S I N G
R   A        Y   R   R   E
I O T A    A S P E C T S
```

Solutions

Page 17
Other possible ideas include a shoebox and a microwave

Page 19

L	I	F	T	S	
I		R		T	V	S
T		A	I	R		P
T	U	G		A	G	O
L		I	O	N		O
E	E	L		G		K
		E	N	E	M	Y

Page 20
Melodramatically uses all the letters. Other words include all, ally, call, cam, car, card, cat, dole, dram, drama, dramatic, dramatically, dray, ear, earl, ill, lard, lay, lea, lemma, lit, mar, maraca, mat, melodrama, melodramatic, melody, rally, ram, ray, tam, till and yard

Page 21

Angers	Ranges
Ardent	Ranted
Avails	Saliva
Burble	Rubble
Deafer	Feared
Deeper	Peered
Eighth	Height
Erased	Seared
Ethics	Itches
Impure	Umpire
Meaner	Rename
Naiver	Ravine
Pierce	Recipe
Pseudo	Souped
Sheets	Theses

Page 22

Reward	Drawer
Strap	Parts
Regal	Lager
Room	Moor

Page 23

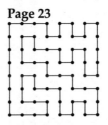

Page 24

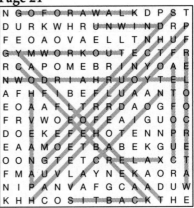

Page 26
29 = 4+2 ×5 −1
38 = 5×4 −1 ×2
44 = 5×2 +1 ×4

Page 27
Bed: grabbed / bedroom
Pens: dampens / pension
Gate: tailgate / gateway

Solutions

Page 29

	C	E		R		B		
	A	X		O	B	E	Y	
S	U	I	T	A	B	L	Y	
	S	N	R		S	O	O	T
	E	T	A		O	N	O	
A	S	H		E		D	D	T
	E	R	R	S		D		
	M	O	A		S	O	S	
F	L	A	W		T	A	U	T
	I	A	N		N	B	A	
L	Y	N	N		S	E	T	T

Page 30

44	11	77	7	21	50	19	66
21	3	2	16	12	26	13	62
34	70	35	61	60	45	15	5

Page 31

Possible words include lead, liar, load, lord, pear, tead, tear, toad, told and torr

Page 32

Climbing, question, trivially, opaque and minimum

Page 33

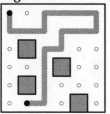

Page 34

Page 36

Organizer uses all the letters. Other words include ago, argon, ego, eon, ergo, gone, goner, gore, gorier, groan, ignore, ion, iron, nor, oar, oaring, ogre, one, orange, ore, organ, razor, region, roan, roar, roaring, roe, roger, zero, zeroing and zone

Page 37

28	−	6	= 22	63	÷ 9	= 7
53	+	6	= 59	45	+ 18	= 63
8	+	35	= 43	11	+ 16	= 27
60	÷	5	= 12	9	× 8	= 72
8	×	10	= 80	11	× 12	= 132
44	÷	4	= 11	40	− 13	= 27
64	−	16	= 48	35	÷ 5	= 7
108	÷	9	= 12	9	× 9	= 81
9	×	2	= 18	11	× 11	= 121
11	×	5	= 55	3	× 2	= 6

Solutions

Page 39

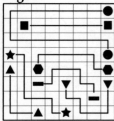

Page 40

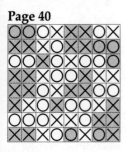

Page 42

Beijing, Kiev, Kuala Lumpur, Miami, Rio de Janeiro, San Francisco

Page 43

A	D	C	E	B
B	E	D	C	A
E	C	B	A	D
D	A	E	B	C
C	B	A	D	E

D	C	B	A	E
A	E	D	C	B
B	A	E	D	C
C	B	A	E	D
E	D	C	B	A

Page 44

Page 45

17 × 5 =	**85**		19 + 72 =	**91**
8 + 51 =	**59**		31 - 16 =	**15**
14 × 7 =	**98**		8 + 29 =	**37**
78 ÷ 2 =	**39**		96 ÷ 12 =	**8**
8 + 58 =	**66**		174 ÷ 6 =	**29**
35 - 13 =	**22**		171 ÷ 3 =	**57**
41 - 23 =	**18**		56 - 21 =	**35**
12 × 3 =	**36**		32 + 23 =	**55**
32 - 13 =	**19**		24 + 21 =	**45**
71 + 14 =	**85**		7 × 16 =	**112**

Page 46

Orchid, primrose, geranium, sunflower, delphinium

Page 47

Silhouette D:

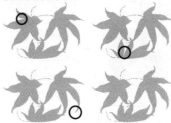

Solutions

Page 48

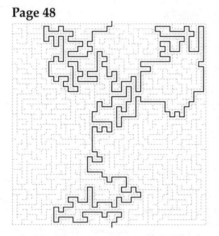

Page 49

Snores, rosewater, theft, enclosure, stags, twit, dawned

Page 50

There are 8 circles:

Page 51

Page 52

51 cubes: 5 on the top level, 12 on the second level, 16 on the third level and 18 on the bottom level

Page 53

The Mindfulness Puzzle Book

Solutions

Page 54

R	W	Y		B		F		E		P
O	R	A	T	E		I	L	L	E	G	A	L
U		R		T		K		A		O		A
T	E	R	M	I	N	I		M	E	S	S	Y
E		A				N		I				E
S	E	N	S	A	T	I	O	N		T	O	R
		T		P				G		W		
M	A	Y		P	R	O	M	O	T	I	O	N
I				R		F				L		E
M	E	T	R	O		F	R	A	G	I	L	E
I		R		V		S		N		G		D
C	L	I	M	A	T	E		O	C	H	R	E
S		O		L		T		N		T		D

Page 55
Words include blasé, brave, bravo, breve, plasm, plate, prase, and prate

Page 57

F	B	E	C	D	A
E	C	D	A	B	F
D	A	B	F	C	E
B	F	C	E	A	D
C	E	A	D	F	B
A	D	F	B	E	C

Page 58

	1	☀	1		☀
0	1	1		2	☀
		1			2
	1	☀	1		☀
1	2			3	2
☀		1	☀	☀	1

Page 60
Other ideas include a book, a handbag and a wrapped sweet

Page 61
Horse, clever, bonus, timely

Page 62
Environmentalism uses all the letters. Other words include environment, environmental, eon, inn, iris, iron, ism, lira, men, mental, mentor, neon, nor, not, oral, rat, roe, rot, sin, sir, tar, taro, toe, ton, tonne, tor and viral

Page 63

19:45 - 15:40 = **04:05**

03:15 - 00:15 = **03:00**

11:45 - 06:05 = **05:40**

08:30 + 09:00 = **17:30**

11:25 + 08:10 = **19:35**

23:20 - 08:15 = **15:05**

10:30 - 06:50 = **03:40**

04:00 + 09:35 = **13:35**

23:20 - 12:15 = **11:05**

01:30 + 01:30 = **03:00**

Page 64

LOUD ⟩ LORD ⟩ LORE ⟩ PORE ⟩ PURE ⟩ PURR

Page 67
Profusely uses all the letters. Other words include elf, fey, floe, floes, flop, flops, flour, flours, floury, flu, flue, flues, fly, foe, foes, fop, fops, for, fore, fores, foul, fouler, fouls, four,

175

Solutions

fours, foyer, foyers, fro, fry, fuel, fuels, fur, furl, furls, furs, fury, fuse, profuse, self, serf, surf and yourself

Page 68

$40 \div 8 = 5$
$55 - 6 = 49$

$66 \div 11 = 6$
$44 - 10 = 34$

$12 \times 9 = 108$
$3 \times 10 = 30$

$121 \div 11 = 11$
$36 + 13 = 49$

$27 - 13 = 14$
$6 \times 10 = 60$

$9 \times 3 = 27$
$5 \div 5 = 1$

$5 \times 10 = 50$
$60 - 10 = 50$

$11 + 65 = 76$
$15 + 1 = 16$

$4 \times 9 = 36$
$10 \times 12 = 120$

$3 \times 3 = 9$
$12 \div 12 = 1$

Page 69

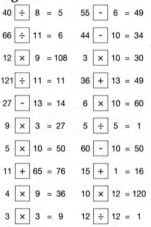

Page 70

Beetroot, mushroom, tomato, cabbage, cucumber

Page 71

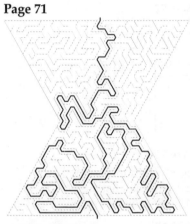

Page 72

	S		P		F	
L	I	B	R	A	R	Y
	C		E		E	
S	K	I	P	P	E	D
	E		A		B	
I	N	E	R	T	I	A
	S		E		E	

Page 73

$116 \div 2 = \mathbf{58}$
$12 \times 13 = \mathbf{156}$

$64 - 5 = \mathbf{59}$
$45 - 27 = \mathbf{18}$

$13 + 39 = \mathbf{52}$
$12 \div 6 = \mathbf{2}$

$44 - 11 = \mathbf{33}$
$2 \times 5 = \mathbf{10}$

$21 - 6 = \mathbf{15}$
$54 - 19 = \mathbf{35}$

$9 + 32 = \mathbf{41}$
$21 + 38 = \mathbf{59}$

$6 + 31 = \mathbf{37}$
$47 - 8 = \mathbf{39}$

$30 + 13 = \mathbf{43}$
$5 \times 16 = \mathbf{80}$

$8 \times 17 = \mathbf{136}$
$45 - 6 = \mathbf{39}$

$95 - 27 = \mathbf{68}$
$12 \times 4 = \mathbf{48}$

Solutions

Page 74

		6		2		
			4			
	4			4	2	2
3				6	4	
8						
		5				
		6				4
	4					

Page 75

Hood: childhood / hoodwink
List: idealist / listless
Mill: treadmill / million

Page 76

A	S	M	B	T	H	T	E	T	L	A	T	P	K	U
D	H	T	A	S	R	S	T	T	E	I	R	S	O	E
U	O	R	O	A	I	A	I	O	S	S	B	O	I	P
C	R	T	O	O	F	B	G	E	R	O	U	R	R	R
K	S	T	T	D	B	G	A	I	R	R	A	O	E	A
O	E	R	L	A	K	R	B	C	R	E	A	G	M	G
N	O	L	R	C	T	H	G	S	H	E	D	P	S	U
T	H	S	I	F	D	L	O	G	Y	B	G	U	N	O
R	O	R	E	T	S	M	A	H	G	N	E	D	I	S
S	R	I	T	R	O	G	O	D	A	F	O	B	U	S
R	G	I	P	A	E	N	I	U	G	C	T	P	I	B
O	R	N	E	R	P	S	C	H	I	C	K	E	N	E
R	A	D	N	I	G	G	L	R	A	E	E	A	I	A
G	E	O	I	N	D	R	D	T	G	R	S	C	K	G
A	U	L	C	O	C	K	A	T	I	E	L	A	O	E

Page 77

21	42	14	56	70	35	5	40

44	59	31	49	7	42	14	12

37	47	2	3	24	6	40	39

Page 78

	C	E		E		R		
	L		A		C	O	I	L
L	E	S	S		O	F	T	
	A	T	T	N		F	U	R
	R	Y	E		A	S	A	P
	E		R		E	L	M	
I	D	S		E	A	T		
	E		A		T	S	A	
U	T	T	E	R		I	M	P
	O		P	L	A	N	E	S
A	R	R	A	Y		G	E	E

Page 79

Beach ball, noodle, recliner, rubber ring, sandcastle, towel

Page 80

Departure, passports, quarantine, announcement

Page 82

3	4	4	0	5	0	5	6
2	6	5	0	1	3	4	1
2	0	4	3	6	1	4	1
2	1	3	3	1	4	5	2
6	5	6	4	1	4	2	5
1	0	3	2	2	0	0	5
6	2	6	6	3	5	0	3

Page 83

Jaguar, hamster, antelope, armadillo, rhinoceros

Page 84

Outvote, votive, above, vibe, added

Page 85

FAST	FACT	FACE	FARE	HARE	HERE

Solutions

Page 86

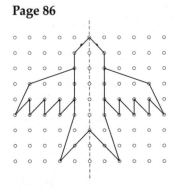

Page 87

Leased   Sealed
Pincer   Prince
Porter   Report
Primes   Simper
Rushes   Ushers

Page 89

Schoolmistresses uses all the letters. Other words include choose, chooses, ire, ires, lose, loses, mire, mires, miser, miss, misses, mist, mistress, mistresses, mists, resist, resists, rim, rims, rise, school, schoolmistress, schools, sir, sire, sires, sis, sol, sols, stress, stresses, tress, tresses, trim and trims

Page 90

$21 = 6{-}2 \times 4 +5$
$31 = 6\times4 +5 +2$
$41 = 4{+}2 \times6 +5$

Page 91

Wolf   Flow
Redraw   Warder
Deliver   Reviled
Peels   Sleep

Page 88

Abodes   Adobes
Adores   Soared
Allure   Laurel
Bosses   Obsess
Budges   Debugs
Creams   Scream
Dashed   Shaded
Filter   Trifle
Girths   Rights
Groans   Organs

Page 92

There are 15 stars:

Solutions

Page 93

	I	N	T	A	K	E	
	L		R			R	
A	L	O	N	E		A	
S		P	N			S	
K		E	V	A	D	E	
E		R				E	
D	R	A	G	O	N		

Page 95

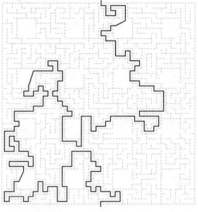

Page 96

	A	B	B	O	T		C	E	A	S	E	D
I		A	R		S		A		T		Y	
D	E	S	I	G	N	E	R	S		R	Y	E
E		E	A		R		E		A		S	
A	R	S	O	N		I	N	D	E	N	T	
S			I		O			G				
	D	I	S	C	O	U	R	A	G	E	D	
	L			S		B				A		
S	L	O	G	A	N		S	O	L	I	D	
Z		N		L		E		O		Y		A
E	W	E		O	B	S	E	R	V	I	N	G
T		S		R		S		B		N		E
A	S	S	A	Y	S		U	S	A	G	E	

Page 97

Suitcase	Briefcase
Sunglasses	Sun hat
Hotel booking	Motel booking
Sun block	Moisturizer
Wallet	Comb
Train ticket	Car park ticket
Driving licence	Driving glasses

Page 99

	F		S		D		O		
	O		T		A	U	R	A	
E	X	P	O		U	N	I		
	T	R	O	U	B	L	E	S	
	R	O	G			O	N	E	
	O	M	E	N		A	T	E	
W	T	O		I		D	A	N	
		T	A	G	S		T		
	H	I	G	H		G	I	S	
		O	U	T	L	O	O	K	
M	I	N	E	S		D	N	A	

Page 100

Other ideas include a cake, cookie and apple.

Page 101

Moon: honeymoon / moonlight
Sleep: oversleep / sleepwalk
Works: fireworks / workshop

Solutions

Page 102

Page 103

Underplay uses all the letters. Other words include dual, due, duel, duly, dun, dune, dupe, laud, launder, laundry, lunar, lure, lured, neural, nude, penury, plunder, prude, prune, pruned, pun, puny, pure, purely, purl, purled, rude, rudely, rue, rued, rule, ruled, run, rune, ulna, ulnae, under, underlay, unread, unready, unreal, upend, upland, urn, urned and yule

Page 104

43 + 4 = 47   16 − 4 = 12

6 + 40 = 46   6 × 12 = 72

72 ÷ 8 = 9   78 + 7 = 85

57 + 2 = 59   20 + 10 = 30

12 ÷ 12 = 1   30 − 13 = 17

56 − 16 = 40 12 + 19 = 31

2 + 16 = 18   6 × 3 = 18

4 × 8 = 32   88 ÷ 8 = 11

5 × 10 = 50   10 × 6 = 60

5 + 34 = 39   16 + 64 = 80

Page 105

Stylus, wallow, topknot, newton, recur, defused, sixes

Page 107

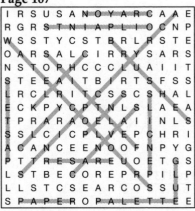

Solutions

Page 109

3	2	4	1		4	3	1	2		4	2	3	1		2	3	4	1
4	1	2	3		1	2	4	3		3	1	2	4		1	4	3	2
2	3	1	4		2	4	3	1		2	4	1	3		3	1	2	4
1	4	3	2		3	1	2	4		1	3	4	2		4	2	1	3

Page 110

9	63	7	51	50	75	25	**5**

19	53	43	62	31	11	22	**2**

33	71	51	67	35	5	9	**3**

Page 111

Cyclone, monsoon, heatwave, hurricane, precipitation

Page 112

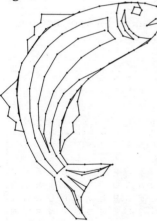

Page 113

7	5	4	2	6	1	3
3	6	2	1	7	4	5
2	7	5	6	4	3	1
4	3	7	5	1	2	6
1	2	6	4	3	5	7
5	1	3	7	2	6	4
6	4	1	3	5	7	2

Page 114

Maximum, television, equatorial, cubic, apparel

Page 115

E		I		P				U		C		E
S	O	C	K	E	T	S		P	L	U	G	S
O		O		P		T		K		L		P
T	E	N		P	R	E	S	E	N	T	L	Y
E				E		R		E		U		
R	U	L	E	R		E	M	P	E	R	O	R
I		A				O		A		E		
C	O	N	N	E	C	T		L	I	L	A	C
		D		X		Y		Y		A		
W	A	L	L	P	A	P	E	R		E	E	L
R		O		A		E		I		L		L
A	P	R	O	N		D	E	C	L	A	R	E
P		D		D				S		N		D

Page 117

17 + 79 =	**96**	28 + 32 =	**60**
5 × 10 =	**50**	14 × 3 =	**42**
25 + 18 =	**43**	5 × 16 =	**80**
56 - 9 =	**47**	31 + 12 =	**43**
27 + 10 =	**37**	6 × 4 =	**24**
87 - 23 =	**64**	29 - 21 =	**8**
43 - 25 =	**18**	17 × 6 =	**102**
11 × 15 =	**165**	5 × 7 =	**35**
12 × 15 =	**180**	10 × 4 =	**40**
73 - 6 =	**67**	172 ÷ 4 =	**43**

Solutions

Page 118

	R		I		H		R	
	E		D		A	F	A	R
V	A	N	I	S	H	E	D	
	L	E	O		A	D	A	M
	I	T	C	H		O		E
	S		Y		E	R	S	T
L	T	D		T		A	C	E
	I	R	I	S			A	
	C	A	T	A	C	O	M	B
		P	E	R	H	A	P	S
A	H	E	M		E	P	I	C

Page 119

Lettuce, carrot, artichoke, parsnip, broccoli

Page 120

Varnished uses all the letters. Other words include advise, adviser, aver, avers, avid, dervish, diva, divan, divans, divas, dive, diver, divers, dives, drive, driven, drives, have, haven, havens, haves, hive, hived, hives, invade, invader, invaders, invades, naive, nave, naves, navies, rave, raved, raven, ravens, raves, ravine, ravined, ravines, ravish, ravished, rev, revs, rive, riven, rives, save, saved, saver, shave, shaved, shaver, shiver, shrive, shriven, vain, vainer, van, vane, vanes, vanish, vanished, vans, varied, varies, varnish, vase, vein, veins, vend, vends, via, viand, viands, vie, vied, vies, vine, vines, visa

Page 123

Page 124

	1		🌑	🌑	1
2	🌑	2		3	
🌑	3		2	🌑	2
	🌑	2	4	🌑	4
	2	🌑	3	🌑	🌑
					2

Page 125

Imagine, mindful, smile, finish

Page 126

		M	E	T	R	O
C	H	A		R		N
O		J	O	I	N	S
N		O		N		P
C	O	R	G	I		E
U		C		T	I	C
R	E	A	D	Y		

Page 127

Words include aced, acid, aped, apex, arid, edge, épée, iced and ired

Solutions

Page 128

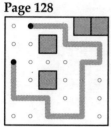

Page 130

Falcon, sparrow, seagull, blackbird, woodpecker

Page 132

L	G	S	S	S	K	A	L	B	G	M	C	K	U	A
I	U	L	W	R	S	S	I	L	R	B	W	R	B	S
N	K	R	I	S	G	L	I	C	E	C	R	E	A	M
I	M	H	M	R	L	N	N	T	G	K	E	V	T	A
H	N	H	M	E	O	L	I	M	A	L	R	T	H	T
H	I	E	I	N	L	K	E	R	A	A	L	O	I	T
K	S	I	N	I	S	T	S	H	R	H	B	B	N	S
S	U	N	G	L	A	S	S	E	S	E	E	I	G	S
E	N	R	C	C	L	T	N	A	V	A	B	S	T	B
M	S	S	L	E	W	O	T	H	C	A	E	B	R	S
B	H	M	E	R	E	M	I	H	R	D	W	S	U	E
V	I	E	E	T	I	A	B	I	K	I	N	I	N	R
R	N	R	K	L	I	A	S	A	E	R	W	A	K	R
H	E	B	A	L	L	E	R	B	M	U	N	U	S	S
D	A	I	B	L	L	S	R	N	S	O	N	I	R	H

Page 133

10 × 7 =	**70**	25 + 82 =	**107**
135 ÷ 5 =	**27**	12 × 8 =	**96**
9 × 7 =	**63**	20 + 98 =	**118**
28 + 9 =	**37**	65 - 16 =	**49**
57 + 12 =	**69**	63 - 11 =	**52**
172 ÷ 2 =	**86**	32 - 28 =	**4**
26 - 20 =	**6**	88 - 19 =	**69**
26 + 38 =	**64**	26 + 87 =	**113**
87 - 6 =	**81**	46 - 28 =	**18**
9 × 17 =	**153**	58 + 10 =	**68**

Page 134

Possible words include bland, bleed, blend, blind, brand, bread, bream, breed, brine, build, dread, dreed, dried, gland, gleam, grand, greed, grind, guild and guile

Page 135

Other ideas include a mountain and a pair of crossing trees

Page 137

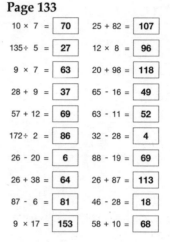

Page 138

TIME	TILE	TILL	TOLL	TOLD	GOLD

Solutions

Page 139

Desserts	Stressed
Mined	Denim
Stink	Knits
Smart	Trams

Page 140

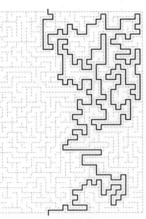

Page 144

D	B	C	E	A
E	C	A	B	D
A	D	E	C	B
C	A	B	D	E
B	E	D	A	C

A	B	E	D	C
D	E	C	B	A
C	A	D	E	B
E	C	B	A	D
B	D	A	C	E

Page 145

Adverb	Braved
Anoint	Nation
Danger	Garden
Deeply	Yelped
Equals	Squeal
Equips	Piques
Ingest	Tinges
Inners	Sinner
Meteor	Remote
Neural	Unreal
Opuses	Spouse
Rawest	Waters
Resets	Steers
Return	Turner
Review	Viewer

Page 141

Cast: broadcast / castaway
Power: manpower / powerboat
Drift: snowdrift / driftwood

Page 142

Responsibilities uses all the letters. Other words include bit, bite, bites, bits, ester, ibis, ire, ires, its, lie, lies, lire, lit, nest, nose, one, ones, pone, pones, pose, post, poster, psst, rite, rites, set, sets, son, sons, sop, sops, stir, tie, ties, tire and tires

Solutions

Page 146

81	÷	9	= 9		5	×	5	= 25
20	-	13	= 7		144	÷	12	= 12
20	+	9	= 29		48	÷	6	= 8
35	÷	5	= 7		3	+	21	= 24
39	-	3	= 36		16	+	34	= 50
3	÷	3	= 1		9	×	7	= 63
53	-	12	= 41		7	×	11	= 77
2	+	36	= 38		17	+	19	= 36
8	×	6	= 48		27	-	6	= 21
56	÷	7	= 8		59	-	12	= 47

Page 147

	N	O	R	M	A	L
	E		S			O
O	R	B	I	T	A	L
	V					N
N	E	P	T	U	N	E
E			A			O
T	R	E	N	D	Y	

Page 148

	8					
	8			8		
3	6			3		
				6	4	
						2
	2			4	2	2
	2			4		

Page 149

Other ideas include a sandwich and a pair of trousers

Page 150

Page 151

Cosmetic, diamond, tuft, nylon, haunch, cynic, alumna

Page 152

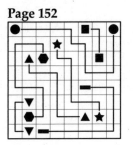

Solutions

Page 153

17:50 - 05:55 =	**11:55**
22:10 - 20:20 =	**01:50**
08:00 + 05:20 =	**13:20**
15:50 + 03:45 =	**19:35**
08:10 + 05:40 =	**13:50**
18:55 - 15:55 =	**03:00**
06:25 - 00:55 =	**05:30**
16:45 + 01:40 =	**18:25**
10:35 - 00:35 =	**10:00**
13:45 - 00:25 =	**13:20**

Page 154

B	A	D	C	F	E
C	E	F	B	A	D
F	D	A	E	C	B
E	C	B	F	D	A
D	F	E	A	B	C
A	B	C	D	E	F

Page 156

Dollar	Dalasi
Ruble	Riyal
Peseta	Lek
Rupee	Rupiah
Kyat	Krona
Dirham	Dinar
Yen	Yuan

Page 157

Page 158

27	9	72	6	3	21	84	22
34	17	65	30	39	13	10	72
38	19	3	39	13	46	23	66

Page 159

Solutions

Page 160

1	6	6	3	3	6	2	2
5	3	4	5	2	1	5	5
4	5	4	1	3	3	4	1
6	3	1	6	6	0	2	2
2	3	4	0	1	0	0	0
0	4	4	5	3	6	6	0
2	5	1	1	4	0	5	2

Page 161

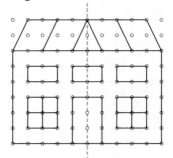

Page 163

	H		P		C		P	
	A		A		O	T	T	O
O	R	B	S		S	E	E	
	M	E	S	S		R		A
	O	A	T		A	R	A	N
A	N	T	H	O	L	O	G	Y
	Y		E		I	R	E	
		T	B	A				B
S	T	R	U	C	T	U	R	E
		I	C	T		F	E	E
B	O	O	K	S	H	O	P	S

Page 164

$$29 = 6 \times 3 + 7 + 4$$
$$59 = 6 + 3 \times 7 - 4$$
$$79 = 6 \times 4 \times 3 + 7$$

Page 165

Willow, coconut, chestnut, sycamore, mountain ash

Page 166

2	6	3	5	7	1	4
1	5	2	4	3	7	6
7	2	6	3	1	4	5
5	7	4	1	6	2	3
6	4	5	7	2	3	1
3	1	7	6	4	5	2
4	3	1	2	5	6	7

Page 167

40 cubes: 3 on the top level, 8 on the second level, 12 on the third level and 17 on the bottom level

Page 168

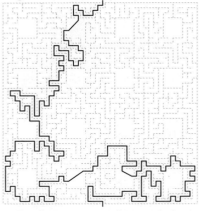

Page 169

LAST 〉 CAST 〉 CART 〉 CARD 〉 WARD 〉 WORD

The Mammoth Book of
Brain Workouts

From the same author,
Dr Gareth Moore

A sharper, smarter brain in just 31 days

Have you ever gone into a room and forgotten why you are there? The synaptic connections between neurons in your brain degenerate with lack of use. So you need to exercise it – and ALL of it, not just a small part. Keep your brain in tip-top condition, and the rest will follow!

This brilliant new puzzle collection has been specially formulated to challenge, stimulate and train all the key different parts of your brain. It's the most complete brain workout programme available, with a whole month's supply of workouts – comprising over 1,000 individual puzzles and exercises.

Each daily workout contains a carefully balanced mixture of puzzles designed to improve your problem solving, to stimulate your creativity, to enhance your concentration, to improve your memory, and to boost your mind power. They'll leave you feeling refreshed and alive.

Visit www.littlebrown.co.uk for more information.

The Mammoth Book of
Logical Brain Games

From the same author,
Dr Gareth Moore

The world's most comprehensive collection of logical puzzles

More than **440** puzzles

Over **60** different types of puzzle

Covering all major types of logic puzzle, this book has everything from Sudoku and Kakuro through to Hanjie and Slitherlink, plus a whole lot more besides such as Tapa, Fences, Yajilin, Nurikabe, Fillomino and many, many others. All of the puzzles use pure logic, requiring no language or cultural knowledge to solve, so the book is suitable for everyone.

Fun and addictive, these puzzles offer a fantastic mental workout. Each of the more than 60 types of puzzle is presented with full instructions in seven carefully graded difficulty levels, from Beginner right through to Master, so whatever your experience you'll find the perfect challenge.

Visit www.littlebrown.co.uk for more information.

The Mammoth Book of
New Sudoku

From the same author,
Dr Gareth Moore

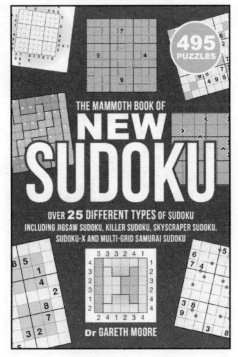

Much more than just a puzzle book

A comprehensive collection featuring every significant variant ever created

Over **25** major Sudoku types

Nearly **150** different variants

Almost **500** puzzles, all created especially for this book, including Jigsaw Sudoku, Killer Sudoku and multi-grid Samurai Sudoku

No other collection of Sudoku comes close – this is without doubt the most definitive volume of Sudoku variants ever compiled, with full instructions and solutions included throughout.

Visit www.littlebrown.co.uk for more information

The Mammoth Book of
Fun Brain Training

From the same author,
Dr Gareth Moore

Ebook edition

A one-of-a-kind full-colour brain training ebook with brand new content

Updated from cover to cover, a third of the original printed book's content has been modified or replaced so that the book can be used without requiring you to write on the page. The original instructions have additionally been rewritten for ebook use.

Bonus downloadable content is also included, with live links in the book that take you to additional creative tasks derived from those in the original edition of the book.

A few minutes a day of FUN BRAIN TRAINING can bring lasting improvement to:

Memory, Logic and Reasoning
Visual and Spatial Awareness
Word and Language Skills
Number Skills

Available now for all colour ebook readers and ebook apps.
Visit www.littlebrown.co.uk for more information.

The Mammoth Book of
Brain Games

From the same author,
Dr Gareth Moore

One Year To A Better Brain!

A fun program featuring LOGIC, OBSERVATION, NUMBER, WORD puzzles and more

78 entirely different types of puzzle

52 weeks of **daily** content

Features over **300** puzzles, all created especially for this book, plus weekly 'Re-Thinking' pages that feature a range of suggestions and ideas to help improve your memory and unleash your creativity, challenging you to make better use of your brain in your daily life.

A scoring system helps to keep you motivated as you improve week by week, with the final page of each week's puzzle offering you the chance to find your BRAIN RANK.

Visit www.littlebrown.co.uk for more information